SELF LOVE FOR WOMEN

Learn How to Find Happiness, Create a Healthy Lifestyle and Develop Self Confidence

MATILDA HART

MW00932716

Copyright © 2023 Matilda Hart. All rights reserved.

The content in this book may not be reproduced, duplicated, or transmitted without direct written permission from the author or publisher.

Under no circumstances will any blame or legal responsibility be held against the publisher, or author, for any damages, reparation, or monetary loss due to the information contained within this book. Either directly or indirectly.

Legal Notice:

This book is copyright protected. It is only for personal use. You cannot amend, distribute, sell, use, quote, or paraphrase any part of the content within this book without the consent of the author or publisher.

Disclaimer Notice:

Please note the information contained within this document is for educational and entertainment purposes only. All effort has been expended to present accurate, up-to-date, reliable, and complete information. No warranties of any kind are declared or implied

Readers acknowledge that the author is not engaged in the rendering of legal, financial, medical, or professional advice. The content within this book has been derived from various sources. Please consult a licensed professional before attempting any techniques outlined in this book.

By reading this document, the reader agrees that under no circumstances is the author responsible for any losses, direct or indirect, that are incurred as a result of the use of the information contained within this document, including, but not limited to, errors, omissions, or inaccuracies.

TABLE OF CONTENTS

A GIFT FOR YOU

Thank you so much for purchasing my book!

Your support means the world to me and I'm truly honored that you have chosen to use my book as part of your self-development journey!

To show you how much I appreciate your support, here's a little thank you gift for you.

A bonus audiobook version of "Self-Love guide book for women" Scan the QR code below to access the Audiobook Version:

PROLOGUE

"Self-love is not selfish; you cannot truly love another until you know how to love yourself." -Unknown

Hey there, girlfriend! I am so excited to dive into this book with you because let's face it, we all need a little bit more self-love in our lives. Am I right?

Now, before we get started, let me ask you a question. Have you ever been on an airplane and heard the flight attendant go through the safety instructions? You know, the part where they tell you to put your oxygen mask on first before assisting others?

Well, self-love is kind of like that. We need to take care of ourselves first so that we can show up as our best selves for those around us. As women, we tend to put everyone else's needs before our own, leaving us feeling drained, exhausted, and unfulfilled. That's why we need to think about the importance of self-love for women, and that's what this book is about. We're going to explore what self-love really means, why it's so crucial for our well-being, and most importantly, how we can start loving ourselves a little bit more every day.

The Importance of Self-Love

You might think that self-love isn't that important, but the truth is, it affects every aspect of our lives. Practicing self-love has a positive impact on our relationships. When we learn to love and accept ourselves, we become more confident and self-assured, which in turn makes us more attractive to others. Research has shown that self-love is linked to higher levels of relationship satisfaction and lower levels of jealousy and conflict (Simpson, Collins, Tran & Haydon, 2007). So if you want to improve your relationships, loving yourself is a good place to start!

Self-love has a significant impact on our mental health. In fact, studies have found that self-compassion, which is a key component of self-love, is associated with lower levels of anxiety and depression (Neff & McGehee, 2010). When we're kinder to ourselves and treat ourselves with the same care that we would give to a friend, we're better equipped to handle life's challenges and bounce back from setbacks.

Our well-being would not be nearly as positive if it weren't for self-love. It's linked to greater life satisfaction, higher self-esteem, and a more positive outlook on life (Huang, Dong, Lu, & Ai, 2019). Living your best life is almost dependent on loving yourself.

Self-love is not just a feel-good concept. It has a real impact on our relationships, mental health, and overall well-being. So let's embrace it and start treating ourselves with the love and kindness we deserve!

My Story with Self-Love

I'm sure you're asking why you should listen to me in the first place. "How do you know what you're talking about? You expect me to just blindly trust you?" Well, let me tell you, I am the perfect person to be writing a book about self-love for women. And no, it's not just because I have a great sense of humor and stunning wit (although that certainly helps).

You see, I've been through the wringer when it comes to self-love. I've spent years putting everyone else's needs before my own, always trying to be the perfect daughter, sister, friend, and partner. But it wasn't until I hit rock bottom that I realized something had to change.

So, I went on a journey of self-discovery, exploring different practices and techniques for cultivating self-love. I read countless books, attended workshops, and worked with coaches and therapists to help me along the way. Let me tell you, it was life changing. Learning to love and accept myself has transformed every aspect of my life, from my relationships to my career, to my overall happiness and well-being. I'm here to share everything I've learned so you don't have to go through the grueling journey that I did.

But you don't have to just take my word for it. I've also got the credentials to back up my expertise. I hold a degree in psychology and have worked as a coach and counselor for women for over a decade. Plus, I'm constantly staying up-to-date on the latest research and practices in the field of self-love and personal growth.

So, whether you're a seasoned self-love pro or just dipping your toes in the water, I've got the knowledge, experience, and humor to guide you on your journey. Let's do this thing!

Setting the Stage

So, now that we've gotten the introductions out of the way, let's talk about what this book is all about and what you, the reader, can expect from this transformative journey.

First and foremost, this book is not just about reading a few chapters and moving on with your life. No, no, no. This book is a journey, a journey of self-discovery, self-love, and personal growth.

Think of it like taking a road trip. You don't just jump in the car and arrive at your destination in five minutes. No, you take the time to enjoy the ride, exploring new places and learning along the way.

That's exactly what this book is all about. We're going to take a journey together, exploring different aspects of self-love and personal growth and discovering new tools and practices that will transform your life. But let me tell you, this journey is not always going to be easy. Just like any road trip, there may be bumps in the road, detours, and unexpected challenges. But that's okay. In fact, those challenges are where real growth and transformation will happen.

So, if you're ready to embark on this transformative journey, buckle up and get ready for an adventure. I can't wait to see where this takes us. In the first chapter, we're going to talk about understanding self-love and what that means for you. But before we do that, we have some formalities to cover really quick.

Copyright Information:

All content in this book is the sole property of the author and may not be reproduced or redistributed without written permission. This includes text, images, and any other content within the book.

Privacy Policy:

We respect your privacy and are committed to protecting your personal information. Any personal information collected during the purchase or use of this book will be used solely for the purpose of delivering the book to you and providing any necessary customer service.

We do not sell, share or distribute any personal information to third parties without your express consent, unless required by law.

If you have any concerns or questions about our privacy policy, please don't hesitate to contact us. We're here to ensure your experience with this book is positive and fulfilling.

Now, back to the journey!

CHAPTER 1

UNDERSTANDING SELF-LOVE

"To love oneself is the beginning of a lifelong romance." -Oscar Wilde

This quote emphasizes that self-love is not a one-time event, but rather a lifelong journey. When we learn to love ourselves, we embark on a journey of self-discovery, growth, and inner fulfillment.

Despite its importance for overall well-being, self-love can be a challenging concept to grasp. As women, we are bombarded with societal expectations, gender roles, and external pressures that can make it difficult to prioritize our own needs and desires.

In this chapter, we will delve into the multifaceted concept of self-love, explore the differences between self-love and narcissism, and unpack the various internal and external barriers that can impede our journey towards self-love.

Self-Love, a Multifaceted Concept

Self-love is like a beautiful gem with many facets, each representing a different aspect of this empowering concept. It's not just about a superficial, ego-driven love; it goes much deeper than that. Self-love encompasses various dimensions that contribute to our overall well-being and happiness that can be split into six categories: self-acceptance, self-compassion, self-care, self-worth, self-trust, and self-esteem.

Self-Acceptance

One vital aspect of self-love is self-acceptance. This is the act of embracing all of our glorious imperfections and quirks. It's like giving yourself a big, warm hug and saying, "Hey, I'm flawed and that's okay!

Self-acceptance is all about recognizing that perfection is a myth and that we're all beautifully flawed in our unique ways. It's not about settling or giving up on growth, but rather acknowledging that we're all works in progress and that's perfectly fine.

When we learn to accept ourselves, flaws and all, we free ourselves from the burden of constantly striving to be someone we're not. We can start to focus on our strengths and appreciate all that we have to offer instead of tearing ourselves down with negative self-talk.

The best part? When we learn to accept ourselves, we open the door to accepting and loving others more fully. It's a beautiful ripple effect that starts with us.

Self-Compassion

You know how we can be our own worst critic sometimes? We beat ourselves up for the smallest mistakes and set impossibly high standards that we can never meet. Well, self-compassion is the opposite. Instead, it's about treating ourselves with the same kindness, concern, and support that we would offer to a good friend who is struggling.

Self-compassion involves three key elements: self-kindness, common humanity, and mindfulness. Self-kindness is all about treating ourselves with warmth, understanding, and forgiveness. Instead of berating ourselves for our flaws and failures, we offer ourselves comfort and reassurance.

Common humanity is the idea that we are not alone in our struggles and that everyone experiences pain and suffering at times. When we recognize that our experiences are part of the human condition, it can help us feel less isolated and more connected to others.

Finally, mindfulness is the ability to observe our thoughts and feelings without judgment or avoidance. It's about acknowledging our pain and discomfort, but also recognizing that they are temporary and don't define us as individuals.

Self-Care

Self-care is a crucial component of self-love. It's about nourishing our physical, mental, and emotional well-being through practices like proper nutrition, exercise, restful sleep, engaging in hobbies and setting healthy boundaries. Taking care of ourselves allows us to replenish our energy and maintain a healthy balance in life.

It's about taking care of yourself physically, mentally, and emotionally. You know, like when you finally get around to drinking enough water and actually remembering to put on sunscreen. Or maybe it's taking a break from work to read a good book or go for a walk.

Let's not forget the ultimate act of self-care: saying no to that toxic friend who always drains your energy. Self-care is all about putting yourself first and making sure your own needs are met. It's not selfish; it's necessary. So go ahead, indulge in that bubble bath and treat yourself to that slice of cake. You deserve it, babe.

Self-Worth

Self-worth, oh self-worth. The elusive and yet so important concept. Self-worth is all about how we see ourselves and the value we place on our own existence. When we have a healthy sense of self-worth, we're more confident, we make better decisions, and we don't let the opinions of others shake us. On the other hand, when our self-worth is low, we might feel like we don't deserve good things in life, or we might settle for less than we deserve. It's like wearing a pair of glasses that distorts our view of ourselves, and it can be hard to take them off.

But, here's the thing: self-worth is not something that can be earned or achieved. It's inherent to our being. We don't need to do anything or prove anything to have self-worth. We just need to recognize it and own it.

It's important to cultivate self-worth because it's the foundation of self-love. Without a sense of our own worth, we can't truly love ourselves. And when we love ourselves, we can show up in the world as the best version of ourselves.

Self-Trust

Ah, self-trust - a vital aspect of self-love that is often overlooked. Self-trust means having faith in your own abilities, judgments, and decisions. It involves listening to your inner voice and honoring your intuition. When you trust yourself, you are more confident in your choices, you take risks, and you know that even if things don't go as planned, you'll be able to handle it.

It's easy to lose trust in ourselves when we make mistakes or experience failures. We may start to doubt our abilities and feel insecure about our decisions. However, self-trust is essential for personal growth and self-love. When we trust ourselves, we are more resilient, we bounce back from setbacks, and we are able to take on new challenges.

Think of a time when you made a decision that turned out to be the right one, despite others' doubts. Maybe you trusted your gut feeling and it led you in the right direction, or you trusted your own judgment and made a decision that others disagreed with, but it turned out to be the best for you. These moments are a testament to the power of self-trust.

Self-Esteem

Self-esteem is like the popular kid in school. Everyone wants to be around them, but not everyone knows how to be friends with them. Similarly, self-esteem is often sought after, but not everyone knows how to build it. Self-esteem is the value we place on our own abilities and worthiness.

Having healthy self-esteem can lead to better mental and physical health, more confidence, and a greater sense of fulfillment in life. On the other hand, low self-esteem can lead to negative self-talk, self-doubt, and even mental health issues like anxiety and depression.

However, building self-esteem isn't just about telling yourself that you're amazing and perfect all the time. It's about acknowledging your strengths and weaknesses, setting realistic goals, and practicing self-compassion.

It's never too late to work on building your self-esteem and improving your relationship with yourself. Remember, you are worthy and deserving of love and respect, and your self-esteem should reflect that.

Now, I know what you might be thinking: "Isn't self-esteem the same as self-worth?" The answer is no and let me tell you why.

Self-esteem and self-worth are related concepts, but they are not the same. Self-esteem is the evaluation of your own abilities and worth based on how they measure up to some standards that you probably made up in your head. It's often related to accomplishments and external factors such as appearance, job performance, and social status. On the other hand, self-worth is a more fundamental sense of personal value that is based on your inherent worth as a human being, regardless of external achievements or circumstances.

So, in the shortest and simplest terms, while they both involve valuing yourself, self-worth is more about valuing who you are as a person, while self-esteem is more about valuing what you do or have accomplished.

It's important to know the different facets of self-love because, well, you can't build a strong and sturdy house with just one brick, can you? Self-love is like that too. It's a foundation built on many bricks, or facets, that work together to give you a solid base. Without each of these important pieces, your foundation can start to crumble and, before you know it, your self-love house comes crashing down. So, let's make sure we know all the pieces of the puzzle so we can build a strong and sturdy foundation for our self-love house.

Understanding the Differences

Have you ever heard the term "self-love" thrown around a lot, but felt a bit confused about what it really means? It's understandable since self-love, as you've just learned, is a multifaceted concept that's sometimes confused with other things like narcissism or self-care. Let's take a closer look at what self-love really means and how it differs from other related concepts. By understanding these differences, you can learn how to cultivate a healthy sense of self-love that allows you to embrace and celebrate all aspects of yourself. So let's dive in!

Self-Love vs. Narcissism

It's an age-old question, and something you might struggle with when you're trying to love yourself. You might ask yourself, "doesn't loving myself just make me an egotistical narcissist? The answer is no, and there are a lot of reasons why this couldn't be further from the truth.

While both concepts may involve focusing on yourself, there is a crucial difference between the two. Self-love is about recognizing and embracing all parts of ourselves, including the vulnerabilities and imperfections, while narcissism involves an inflated sense of self-importance, coupled with a lack of empathy for others.

Let's say you're preparing for an important job interview. With self-love, you would take steps to boost your self-confidence and self-acceptance. You might remind yourself of your past successes and positive qualities and reassure yourself that you're worthy and capable of success.

On the other hand, if you were a narcissist, you would become fixated on your own importance and view other applicants as inferior. You exaggerate your abilities or accomplishments to make yourself appear superior and disregard the feelings or needs of others in pursuit of your own goals. As a narcissist, you know that you'll crush the interview without preparation because there's no one who's more fit for the job than you.

Do you see the difference there? Self-love is about valuing yourself, flaws and all, while narcissism is about inflating your self-importance to the point where you don't have flaws at all. In addition, self-talk that comes from self-love focuses on building yourself up, while narcissistic self-talk usually involves tearing others down to make yourself feel better.

Research shows that narcissism is associated with negative outcomes like lower life satisfaction, reduced emotional well-being, and poorer relationship quality. (Konrath, et al., 2014). In contrast, self-love is linked to greater resilience, healthier relationships, and increased well-being, like you've already read. You can easily embrace self-love while steering extra, extra clear of narcissism.

Self-Love vs. Self-Care

Again, both of these concepts can look similar from the outside looking in, but they have distinct differences. They both involve taking care of yourself, that much is true. However, self-love encompasses a holistic and empowering approach to self-acceptance, self-compassion and self-worth, while self-care is more focused on specific activities or practices for well-being. These are things like getting enough sleep, eating well, and engaging in hobbies. They make us feel more rested, nourished, and fulfilled, but they don't make us love ourselves.

Self-love goes beyond these activities to create a deeper sense of inner fulfillment. Self-care is an important aspect of self-love, but you need to combine it with other things to get there. By embracing self-love, we're cultivating a mindset that positively impacts every aspect of our lives. It's a foundational element of our overall being, and we incorporate self-care as part of that.

Self-Love vs. Self-Indulgence

Self-indulgence is all about satisfying your immediate desires and impulses, regardless of the long-term consequences. You're seeking pleasure or avoiding discomfort without considering the impact on yourself or others.

On the other hand, self-love is about taking care of yourself in a way that supports your long-term well-being. You're treating yourself with kindness and compassion, making choices that align with your values and goals. Oftentimes, self-love involves doing things that you don't necessarily *want* to do, while self-indulgence is things that you *want* to do, even if it's not necessarily what you *should* do.

So, while self-indulgence can often lead to short-term gratification, it can also leave you feeling empty and unfulfilled. Self-love, on the other hand, can help you build a sense of inner peace, confidence, and purpose that can last a lifetime.

Self-Love vs. Self-Confidence

Oh boy, self-love vs self-confidence, it's like trying to tell apart identical twins! At first glance, they might seem the same, but they're totally different!

Self-confidence is all about believing in your own abilities and feeling good about what you can do. It's like the cheerleader on your shoulder telling you that you can do anything you set your mind to! Self-confidence is a powerful feeling that can help you overcome challenges and take on the world!

On the other hand, self-love is more about accepting yourself, flaws and all. It's about recognizing your own worth and treating yourself with kindness and respect, even when things aren't going as planned. Self-love is like having a best friend who always has your back, no matter what!

So, while self-confidence is like the loud and proud big sister who can help you conquer the world, self-love is like the wise and gentle aunt who reminds you that you're amazing just the way you are. They might seem similar, but they each bring something unique to the table.

Okay, so now you know what self-love really is, so why is it so dang hard to do? Let's talk about why women struggle with self-love.

Why Women Struggle with Self-love

Let's face it: women often have a harder time loving themselves than men do. While both men and women can struggle with low self-esteem and negative self-talk, studies have shown that women are more likely to experience these issues, especially when it comes to body image. Here are a few reasons why.

Societal Expectations

Women are bombarded with messages from the media, advertising, and even their own peers that promote a certain ideal of beauty and femininity. These messages can be unrealistic and unattainable for many women, and they can lead to feelings of inadequacy and self-doubt. When women feel like they don't measure up to these expectations, it can be hard to love themselves for who they are. Women who are exposed to images of thin models and actresses report lower body satisfaction and higher levels of anxiety and depression (Grabe, Ward, & Hyde, 2008).

We live in a society that often tells women they have to look and act a certain way to be accepted and loved. From a young age, girls are bombarded with images of "perfect" bodies and faces that are often unrealistic and unattainable. This creates a toxic cycle of self-doubt and low self-esteem that can be hard to break. On top of that, women are often expected to put others' needs before their own, which can make it difficult to prioritize self-care and self-love. But here's the thing: you deserve to love yourself just the way you are, regardless of what anyone else says or thinks.

I'm sure you can think of a time when these types of expectations have affected you. Think about what was said to you and who said it. The truth is, it happens to us all the time, and it inevitably impacts our well-being.

Comparison Culture

Social media has made it easier than ever to compare ourselves to others, and women are especially prone to this. Whether it's comparing our bodies, our careers, or our relationships to those of our peers, this constant comparison can erode our sense of self-worth and make it harder to love ourselves as we are.

A study published in the journal *Cyberpsychology, Behavior, and Social Networking* found that women are more likely than men to compare themselves to others on social media, and that this can lead to feelings of envy and decreased self-esteem (Vogel, Rose, Roberts, & Eckles, 2014).

There have been times in my life where I've found myself scrolling through social media, feeling envious of other people's seemingly perfect lives and accomplishments. I've caught myself thinking, "Why can't I be as successful as her?" or "Why don't I have a body like hers?" It's a slippery slope, and before I know it, I'm feeling down on myself and questioning my own worth.

Gender Roles

Women often face unique challenges and stressors in their lives, such as discrimination, harassment, and gender-based violence. These experiences can take a toll on our self-esteem and make it harder to believe in ourselves and our abilities.

A report by the World Health Organization found that violence against women is a global health problem that affects approximately one in three women worldwide (WHO, 2013). This can lead to physical and psychological harm that can impact self-esteem and self-worth. Take Samantha's story for example.

Samantha had a vibrant spirit and dreams as vast as the sky. She radiated confidence and self-love, cherishing her worth and embracing her uniqueness. However, her journey took an unexpected turn when she became a victim of gender-based violence.

Samantha's world was shattered, and the trauma she endured deeply wounded her sense of self-love. The abuse left her questioning her worth and feeling undeserving of love and respect. She blamed herself, believing that she had somehow invited this pain into her life.

As time passed, Samantha's self-esteem crumbled, and the vibrant spirit she once possessed dimmed. She internalized the negative messages from her abuser and society, struggling to see her own strength and beauty. The violence she experienced had not only violated her body but had also scarred her soul.

However, Samantha's journey of healing and self-love began when she found the courage to reach out for support. She connected with organizations and support networks that specialized in helping survivors of gender-based violence. In these safe spaces, she encountered other women who had experienced similar hardships and had found their way back to self-love.

Through therapy, counseling, and the loving embrace of a community, Samantha began to unravel the layers of self-doubt and self-blame. She learned that the violence she experienced was never her fault and that she deserved compassion, respect, and healing.

Samantha discovered the power of self-care and self-compassion. She surrounded herself with positive influences and engaged in activities that nourished her mind, body, and soul. Slowly, she rebuilt her self-esteem, rediscovered her passions, and reclaimed her identity.

As Samantha embarked on her healing journey, she also found her voice. She spoke out against gender-based violence, advocating for awareness, prevention, and support for survivors. Through her bravery, she empowered others to break the silence and seek the help they deserved.

Over time, her self-love grew stronger, like a phoenix rising from the ashes. She embraced her scars as symbols of resilience and growth, understanding that her worth was never defined by the violence she endured but by the love and strength she carried within.

Samantha's story serves as a reminder that despite the immense challenges posed by gender-based violence, healing and self-love are possible. This process takes time, support, and a deep commitment to one's own well-being. Samantha's journey reflects the power of resilience and the transformative nature of self-love, offering hope and inspiration to those who may be on a similar path of healing and self-discovery.

Pause and think about whether there was ever a time when you felt like people's expectations of you as a woman got in the way of what you truly wanted for yourself. You probably have plenty of examples to choose from. This is just one thing that gets in the way of loving yourself and who you are.

Self-Sacrifice

Because of gender role expectations, women are often expected to put the needs of others before their own, whether it's in their personal or professional lives. While caregiving and nurturing can be deeply fulfilling, they can also lead to neglecting our own needs and desires. When we don't prioritize ourselves and our own well-being, it can be hard to truly love and value ourselves.

In fact, women who are primary caregivers for children and elderly relatives are more likely to experience stress and burnout (Sharma, 2013). This can lead to neglecting their own needs and desires, which can impact self-esteem and self-love. I'm not trying to say that you shouldn't love and care for your family and friends, but when it's always expected instead of appreciated, it can take a big toll on you without you even realizing it.

Lack of Representation

Women are often underrepresented in media, politics, and other areas of public life. When we don't see ourselves reflected in the world around us, it can be hard to feel like we belong or are valued. A report by the Geena Davis Institute on Gender in Media found that in family films, male characters outnumbered female characters three to one (Smith, Choueiti, & Pieper, 2013). But is there really any effect on you if there aren't TV show characters that look like you? Surely not. Right?

Meet Maya, a young girl who has always been passionate about science and astronomy. From a young age, she would spend hours reading books about space and dreaming of becoming an astronaut. However, as Maya grew older, she noticed a distinct lack of female scientists and astronauts in the media she consumed.

Maya loved watching movies and TV shows, but she rarely saw women in leading roles as scientists or explorers. Most of the time, women were portrayed as side characters or love interests, reinforcing the notion that science and exploration were primarily male domains. This lack of representation made Maya question whether she could truly pursue her dreams in the field of astronomy.

Seeing this imbalance, Maya's confidence wavered. She started to doubt whether she had what it takes to succeed in a STEM career. It wasn't until she stumbled upon a documentary about female astronauts that Maya's perspective shifted. Seeing women like Mae Jemison, Sally Ride, and Peggy Whitson excel in their fields inspired Maya to believe that she, too, could break barriers and reach for the stars.

Maya's experience highlights the significance of representation in media. When individuals don't see themselves reflected in positive and empowering roles, it can hinder their belief in themselves and limit their aspirations. Fortunately, by showcasing diverse and strong role models, we can inspire future generations and help them realize their full potential, regardless of their gender.

All of these factors can make it challenging for women to practice self-love. However, it's important to remember that self-love is a journey, not a destination. By recognizing these challenges and taking steps to overcome them, women can learn to love themselves more fully and deeply. So what other barriers are there? We've already talked about everything that happens outside our bodies that affects us, and it makes a bunch of little barriers on the inside, things like self-doubt, guilt, and inner criticism.

Internal Barriers

These are the mental and emotional obstacles that can get in the way of us loving ourselves fully and authentically. From self-doubt to negative self-talk, these barriers can make it hard for us to see our own worth and potential. But fear not! By identifying and working to overcome these barriers, we can clear the path to self-love and a happier, more fulfilling life. So, let's dive in and tackle those internal barriers head-on!

Self-Doubt

Self-doubt is the nagging feeling that we're just not measuring up. And unfortunately, it's one of the biggest internal barriers to self-love for women.

Studies have shown that women tend to experience self-doubt more frequently than men. In fact, research has found that women are more likely to underestimate their own abilities and talents, while men are more likely to overestimate theirs (Dunning & Kruger, 1999). This phenomenon is known as the "imposter syndrome," and it can be a major obstacle to developing a healthy sense of self-love.

When we're plagued by self-doubt, it's difficult to believe that we're worthy of love and respect. We may be quick to dismiss compliments or feel like we don't deserve good things that come our way. And worst of all, we may start to believe that the negative voices in our head are telling us the truth.

The truth throughout all of it is this: self-doubt is a liar. It's that friend who always puts us down and tells us we're not good enough. And just like that toxic friend, we need to learn to tune it out and walk away.

Guilt

As women, we can often feel guilty for putting ourselves first or taking time to prioritize our own needs and wants. Self-love and self-care are crucial to our overall well-being and happiness. So, let's explore the impact of guilt on our ability to love ourselves fully and unapologetically.

Research has shown that feelings of guilt can lead to decreased self-esteem and hinder our ability to practice self-love (Tangney, Stuewig, & Mashek, 2007). When we constantly put others' needs before our own and neglect our own self-care, we can start to feel drained, resentful, and unfulfilled.

This is where guilt can creep in, telling us that we're being selfish or that we don't deserve to take time for ourselves, when the reality is that we all deserve love and care.

Inner Criticism

Inner criticism can be a real buzzkill when it comes to self-love. The inner critic never thinks anything you do is good enough, and it loves failure. It's that little voice in your head that tells you that you're not good enough, not pretty enough, not smart enough. Sound familiar?

From a young age, we're bombarded with messages about what we should look like, act like, and achieve. When we fall short of these expectations, our inner critic goes into overdrive, like a zombie that feeds on everything you do wrong in life.

The impact of this inner criticism on our self-love can be significant. It can lead to feelings of inadequacy, self-doubt, and low self-esteem. According to a study published in the *Journal of Personality and Social Psychology*, self-criticism is strongly linked to symptoms of anxiety and depression (Blatt, Zuroff, & Hawley, 2011).

It seems similar to self-doubt, but they aren't the same. While self-doubt is an overall lack of confidence in yourself, inner criticism is more specific and involves negative self-talk and self-judgment. Inner criticism often manifests as an internal voice that is overly harsh, critical, and unforgiving towards yourself. It can lead to feelings of inadequacy, low self-esteem, and self-sabotage.

So, we've talked about self-doubt, guilt, and inner criticism - all the lovely things that can really put a damper on our self-love journey. But why is it important to even acknowledge these internal barriers in the first place?

Well, let me tell you. Recognizing our internal barriers is the first step towards conquering them. It's like taking a magnifying glass to your thoughts and emotions and being able to pinpoint exactly what's holding you back. Once you've done that, you can start to challenge those negative thoughts and beliefs, replacing them with more positive and self-loving ones.

When we acknowledge our internal barriers, we're also able to recognize that we're not alone in this struggle. Every single one of us deals with self-doubt, guilt, and inner criticism from time to time; they are universal human experiences. However, by acknowledging these barriers, we can start to support each other and work together towards self-love and self-acceptance.

So, my lovely friend, let's take a moment to reflect on our own internal barriers and start the process of overcoming them. Let's be kinder to ourselves, challenge those negative thoughts, and celebrate our own unique and wonderful selves. Because at the end of the day, we all deserve to love ourselves fully and completely.

Conclusion

Congrats on making it through this chapter on understanding self-love! Now, if you're ready to take the next step towards becoming the self-love guru you were always meant to be, it's time to dive into the next chapter on building the foundation for self-love. For your convenience, we've included a bulleted list of everything you've learned in this chapter. You're welcome in advance.

In Chapter 2, we'll be talking about practical steps you can take to start cultivating self-love in your daily life. We'll be covering everything from growth mindset practices to boundary setting, so get ready to flex those self-love muscles!

So, don't waste any time! Keep the momentum going and dive into the next chapter. Your relationship with yourself will thank you later!

Takeaways

- The facets of self-love include self-acceptance, self-compassion, self-care, self-worth, self-trust and self-esteem.
- It's important to understand the differences between these facets of self-love, as they all contribute to a healthy sense of self.
- Self-love is not the same as narcissism, self-indulgence, self-confidence, or self-care; these are all surface level things, where self-love works from the inside out.

- Women often struggle with self-love due to societal expectations, comparison culture, and internal barriers such as self-doubt, guilt, and inner criticism.
- Overcoming these internal barriers and building a strong foundation for self-love can lead to a more fulfilling and satisfying life.

CHAPTER 2

BUILDING A FOUNDATION FOR SELF-LOVE

"Love yourself first and everything else falls into line. You really have to love yourself to get anything done in this world." - Lucille Ball.

This quote emphasizes the importance of self-love as the foundation for a fulfilling life. When individuals have a strong foundation of self-love, they are better equipped to navigate challenges and pursue their goals with confidence and resilience. Self-love is a journey that begins with a strong foundation.

In this chapter, we will explore the key building blocks of self-love, from acknowledging our worth and challenging limiting beliefs, to developing self-awareness and a growth mindset. By celebrating our small victories and embracing personal growth, we can lay the groundwork for a fulfilling and empowering journey towards self-love.

Acknowledging Your Worth

Hey there, friend! So, have you ever had one of those days where you just feel like you're not good enough? Like no matter what you do, it's just not up to par? We all have those days, but what if I told you that you have inherent worth just by being you? That's right, you don't have to do anything special to deserve your worth; it's already there!

In this chapter, we're going to talk about building the foundation for self-love, starting with the simple but oh-so-important task of acknowledging your worth. It's time to recognize that you are valuable and deserving of love, no matter what anyone else says or thinks. So, let's dive in and start building that foundation!

Well, first of all, let me just say that you are awesome and amazing just the way you are. But if you want to give yourself a little pat on the back, here are some tips:

1. Make a list of your achievements: Sometimes we forget just how much we've accomplished, so take some time to make a list of all your achievements, big or small. It could be anything from getting good grades in school to learning a new skill or hobby. Go on, do it right now. Get out a journal and title it, "How I'm Going to Love Myself" and make this the first entry.

2. Focus on your strengths: We all have things that we're good at and things that we're not so good at. Instead of dwelling on your weaknesses, focus on your strengths and what makes you unique. Embrace your quirks and talents, and don't be afraid to show them off. Write them down so you can see it on paper!

3. Don't compare yourself to others: It's easy to fall into the trap of comparing yourself to others but remember that everyone has their own unique journey and talents. Comparing yourself to others will only make you feel inadequate and insecure. Focus on your own journey and what makes you special.

4. Get feedback from others: Sometimes it's hard to see our own strengths and achievements, so get feedback from others. Ask your friends, family, or colleagues what they think your strengths are, they can even write it down for you. You might be surprised at what they have to say!

Remember, recognizing your own unique talents and achievements is an important part of building a strong foundation for self-love. So take some time to celebrate yourself and all that you've accomplished!

Challenging Limiting Beliefs and Negative Self Talk

Oh boy, limiting beliefs! These pesky little thoughts that convince us we can't do something or that we're not good enough. They're like a rain cloud that follows us around, raining on our parade. For women, limiting beliefs can be particularly harmful because we're often told from a young age that we can't or shouldn't do certain things because of our gender. And then we internalize these beliefs and they become part of our identity. But guess what? They don't have to be! We can challenge them and change the way we think.

Don't just take my word for it, there are studies that have examined the impact of limiting beliefs on women. One study published in the *Journal of Social and Clinical Psychology* found that women who held negative beliefs about themselves were more likely to experience symptoms of depression and anxiety (Clark & Beck, 2011). The study also found that women who were able to challenge and change these negative beliefs saw improvements in their mental health and well-being.

The science of this suggests that limiting beliefs can have a significant impact on women's mental and physical health, and that challenging and changing these beliefs can lead to improvements in well-being.

Now that we've discussed limiting beliefs and their impact on our self-worth, it's time to take a moment to reflect.

What are some of the limiting beliefs you hold about yourself?

Are they rooted in past experiences or societal expectations?

If you need help coming up with some limiting beliefs, here are some common ones that women tell themselves:

- "I'm not smart/creative/talented enough."
- "I'm not thin/pretty/attractive enough."
- "I'm not worthy of love and affection."
- "I don't deserve success and happiness."
- "I have to put others' needs before my own."
- "I can't do it because I don't have enough experience/skills/knowledge."

These beliefs can be internalized from societal messages, past experiences, or even from personal relationships. It's important to identify and challenge these limiting beliefs in order to build a strong foundation for self-love.

Take some time to identify any negative beliefs you have about yourself and challenge them. Remember, you have the power to change the way you think about yourself. It won't be easy, but it's worth it. Keep reminding yourself of your worth and your unique talents and achievements, and don't let those limiting beliefs hold you back from reaching your full potential.

Okay so you've taken some time to reflect on your own limiting beliefs, but how the heck do you make them stop?

Well, my dear friend, challenging limiting beliefs may not be a walk in the park, but it's worth the effort! Here's my routine for dealing with those annoying, stupid beliefs I have about myself.

Identify The Limiting Belief

The first step is to identify what limiting belief is holding you back. Is it the belief that you're not good enough, smart enough, or talented enough? Once you've identified it, write it down.

You gotta catch that sneaky little voice inside your head that's telling you that you can't do something. You know, the one that says, "I can't do this" or "I'm not good enough for that." Once you hear it, call it out for what it is: a limiting belief. You'll notice that it's a limiting belief if it includes words like "can't, not, won't, isn't," etc.

Examine the Evidence

Ask yourself, "Is this belief based on facts or just my perception?" Look for evidence that supports and contradicts the belief. You'll probably find that there's more evidence that contradicts the belief.

For example, if you have a limiting belief that you're not good enough to apply for a certain job, examine the evidence that supports this belief. Is it based on any actual facts or is it just a feeling of self-doubt? Have you ever received feedback from someone that suggests you're not capable? Here are some questions you can ask yourself to examine the evidence:

- What evidence do I have to support this belief?
- Is this evidence accurate and reliable?
- Are there any other pieces of evidence that contradict this belief?
- Am I jumping to conclusions or making assumptions based on limited information?
- Have I considered all possible explanations for this situation?
- What would someone else say about this situation and my beliefs about it?
- Am I placing too much importance on this belief, and how would things change if I let go of it?

Asking these types of questions can help you challenge your limiting beliefs and gain a more objective perspective on your thoughts and feelings.

Oftentimes, we create limiting beliefs based on assumptions that aren't actually true. By examining the evidence and questioning our assumptions, we can begin to break down these beliefs and replace them with more positive and accurate ones.

Of course, this isn't always an easy process, and it may take time to fully challenge and overcome your limiting beliefs. But remember, self-love is a journey and every step counts!

Reframe the Belief

Once you've examined the evidence, reframe the belief into a positive one. For example, if you believe that you're not smart enough to start your own business, reframe it to "I am intelligent and capable of learning what I need to start my own business."

I know, easier said than done. But it is possible; reframing means taking a more positive and realistic perspective on the situation. Here are some practical tips:

1. Replace negative self-talk with positive affirmations. For example, if your limiting belief is "I'm not good enough", you can reframe it as "I am capable and worthy".

2. Focus on your strengths and past successes. This can help shift your perspective from what you can't do to what you can do.

3. Use humor to reframe the situation. Sometimes a little laughter can go a long way in changing your perspective and making the situation feel less daunting.

4. Get support from others. Sometimes it can be hard to see things clearly when we're stuck in our own negative thought patterns. Talking to a friend, therapist, or coach can help you gain a more balanced perspective.

Sometimes when you're inside a limiting belief, it can be really hard to reframe it into a positive light. Let's talk about some ways you can start practicing incorporating positive affirmations into your life so it becomes second nature for you. That way, you'll be a reframing master!

Practicing Positive Affirmations

Oh boy, it's time to get cheesy and repeat positive statements to ourselves like we're in a cult! Just kidding, affirmations can actually be a helpful tool in building self-love. It's all about choosing statements that resonate with you and repeating them regularly. Yeah, I'm talking about speaking out loud, moving your mouth. And don't worry if it feels awkward or silly at first - you're not alone in feeling that way.

To get started, think about the negative self-talk you tend to engage in and come up with an opposite, positive statement. For example, if you tend to think "I'm not good enough," try saying to yourself, "I am worthy and capable." If you're having difficulty coming up with positive affirmations, you can try a few different things:

1. Look for inspiration: Read books or articles that inspire you, listen to motivational talks, or ask a supportive friend or mentor for help in coming up with positive affirmations.

2. Start small: It can be difficult to shift from negative self-talk to positive affirmations overnight. Start with small, manageable affirmations that feel true to you and work your way up to larger ones.

3. Practice regularly: Practice your affirmations regularly, preferably daily. Repeat them to yourself in the morning, throughout the day, and before bed.

4. Use visual aids: Write your affirmations on sticky notes and place them in visible places, such as on your mirror or computer screen. You can also create a vision board with images that represent your goals and positive affirmations.

Remember, affirmations aren't a magic fix and won't change everything overnight, but with consistent practice, they can help shift your mindset and increase your self-love.

Take Action

Taking action is the best way to challenge limiting beliefs. Start small, and take steps towards your goals, celebrating your achievements no matter how small they may seem. But what does that look like?

Alright, buckle up and let's take a journey towards taking action! First things first, let's identify what action you want to take. Is it signing up for that class you've been eyeing for months? Or maybe finally quitting that job that's been making you miserable? Whatever it is, write it down and get specific about what steps you need to take to make it happen.

Now that you know what you want to do, it's time to take action! Yes, I know, easier said than done. But let's break it down into manageable steps. Start by setting a realistic timeline for yourself. Don't expect to achieve your goal in one day or even one week. Give yourself the time and space to work towards it at a pace that's comfortable for you.

Next, make a plan of action. What do you need to do to make your goal a reality? Break it down into smaller steps and prioritize them. Remember, you don't have to do it all at once. Take it one step at a time.

Now, here comes the hard part - actually taking action! It's normal to feel scared or unsure, but don't let that hold you back. Take that first step and keep moving forward. And don't forget to celebrate the small wins along the way. Did you send that email you've been putting off? Treat yourself to a nice cup of coffee or take a well-deserved break.

Lastly, don't be too hard on yourself if things don't go exactly as planned. Life happens, and sometimes we have to pivot or adjust our plans. Be flexible and adaptable and remember that setbacks are not failures.

So there you have it, folks. Taking action is a journey, but one that's worth it. Trust me, the feeling of accomplishment and pride when you achieve your goal is worth every step.

Congratulations, you gorgeous creature, you! You've learned about the sneaky ways these beliefs can worm their way into your psyche and how to show them who's boss.

Remember, taking action is the key to overcoming these limiting beliefs and unleashing your true potential. So, go out there and kick some limiting belief butt! You got this, girl! But there's another villain to slay: negative self-talk.

Ah, negative self-talk, the pesky little voice inside our heads that just won't shut up. Unlike limiting beliefs, which are deeply held assumptions about ourselves and the world around us, negative self-talk is more like an ongoing internal dialogue that criticizes, doubts, and undermines our sense of self-worth.

It's like having a tiny devil perched on your shoulder, constantly whispering negative thoughts and self-deprecating remarks into your ear. "You're not good enough," "Nobody likes you," "Why bother trying, you'll just fail anyway."

Negative self-talk can be especially problematic for women who are already dealing with a host of external pressures and societal expectations. It can leave us feeling demotivated, insecure, and like we're not living up to some imaginary standard. But fear not, my friend! There are ways to combat negative self-talk and silence that pesky little devil for good.

To battle negative self-talk, you would use the same steps that you would for limiting beliefs but switch the subject to reflect what your mean brain is telling you. Besides that, there are a couple other things to keep in mind when battling negative self-talk:

Practice Self-Compassion

I'm going to get more into this topic in Chapter 3, but here's the main rundown as a facet of self-love. Practicing self-compassion involves being kind, gentle, and understanding towards yourself, especially during moments of pain, failure, or difficulty. It's like being your own supportive best friend who lifts you up when you're feeling down. It's important because negative self-talk can be extremely damaging to our mental health and self-esteem.

One way to practice self-compassion is to talk to yourself the way you would talk to a friend who is going through a tough time. Would you criticize them, put them down, or tell them they're not good enough? Of course not! Instead, you would likely offer words of encouragement, support, and understanding.

Another way to practice self-compassion is to give yourself permission to make mistakes and learn from them. Nobody is perfect, and everyone makes mistakes from time to time. Instead of beating yourself up over them, try to view them as opportunities for growth and learning.

You can also practice self-compassion by taking care of yourself physically, mentally, and emotionally. This could involve things like getting enough sleep, eating well, exercising regularly, practicing mindfulness or meditation, or engaging in hobbies and activities that bring you joy and fulfillment.

Ultimately, the key to practicing self-compassion is to treat yourself with the same kindness, love, and respect that you would offer to others, and I'm going to teach you all about it in Chapter 3. It may take some time and practice to get there, but the more you do it, the easier and more natural it will become.

Use Humor

Using humor is another effective way to battle negative self-talk. It may sound silly, but making fun of yourself or the negative thought can take away its power. Try to think of the negative thought as a ridiculous character in a sitcom and imagine yourself as the witty protagonist who can outsmart it with clever jokes.

For example, if the negative thought is "I'm so dumb, I always make mistakes," you can imagine it as a clumsy cartoon character and say something like "Oops, there goes that silly thought again, tripping over its own feet. Who knew negative self-talk could be so clumsy?"

Of course, it's important to make sure the humor is not at the expense of yourself or others. The goal is to defuse the negative thought and replace it with a more positive and lighthearted perspective.

Surround Yourself With Positivity

Surrounding yourself with positivity can take many forms when practicing self-love. Here are some ways to do so:

1. Identify people who lift you up: Spend time with people who make you feel good about yourself and your accomplishments. Surround yourself with individuals who support and encourage you.
2. Engage in positive self-talk: Practice speaking to yourself positively and give yourself affirmations throughout the day. Encourage yourself to keep going, even when things get tough. Luckily, you just learned how to do that!
3. Consume positive media: Read books, listen to podcasts, and watch shows that are uplifting and empowering. Avoid media that feeds negative self-talk or self-doubt.
4. Cultivate positive environments: Make your home and work environments a positive space by adding decorations or elements that make you feel happy and calm. It seems silly, but it makes a big difference!

Remember, surrounding yourself with positivity is about creating an environment that supports your journey towards self-love. This is something we will talk more about in later chapters, but it's important to introduce you to the tools you'll need for a better life!

Practicing Mindfulness

Practicing mindfulness is a crucial part of self-care, something else you'll learn plenty about in Chapter 3. Practicing mindfulness is all about being fully present and engaged in the moment, without judgment. For women who are trying to cultivate self-love, mindfulness can be a powerful tool to help them stay focused on the present moment and reduce anxiety about the past or future. Mindfulness can take many forms, from meditation to yoga to simply taking a walk outside and paying attention to the sights, sounds, and sensations around you. By incorporating mindfulness practices into your daily routine, you can learn to be more accepting and compassionate toward yourself, which can ultimately lead to a greater sense of self-love and inner peace.

Seeking Outside Help

Sometimes, negative self-talk can progress farther than what we can handle on our own. Seeking professional help can look different for each woman, depending on their individual needs and circumstances. It could involve seeing a therapist or counselor, joining a support group, or seeking guidance from a mentor or trusted friend.

It's important to recognize that seeking professional help is a sign of strength, not weakness. Sometimes we need additional support to work through our struggles and that's okay.

If shame is a barrier to seeking help, it can be helpful to remind ourselves that seeking professional help is a brave and proactive step towards self-improvement. We can also challenge any negative beliefs we may have about seeking help by recognizing the positive impact it can have on our mental and emotional wellbeing.

As a therapist, I've helped countless women overcome negative self-talk, but it wasn't until I confronted my own issues with self-love that I realized how much professional help can truly make a difference. For years, I struggled with an inner critic that told me I wasn't good enough and that I was always falling short. I tried everything from positive affirmations to mindfulness practices, but nothing seemed to work.

Eventually, I mustered up the courage to seek out a therapist myself, and it was the best decision I ever made. With the help of a professional, I was able to identify the root causes of my negative self-talk and develop tools and strategies to combat it. Through therapy, I learned to be kinder and more compassionate to myself, and to let go of the unrealistic expectations I had been holding onto.

I know that seeking professional help can be daunting, and there is often a stigma attached to it. But the truth is, there is no shame in asking for support when we need it. It takes strength to confront our own struggles and to take steps towards healing. And with the right therapist, self-love and acceptance are truly within reach.

Building Self-Awareness

Self-awareness serves as a guiding light that helps us understand our thoughts, emotions, behaviors, and patterns more deeply. By becoming aware of ourselves, we gain valuable insights into what drives us, what triggers our negative self-talk, and what truly matters to us.

Sarah struggles with self-awareness. She often finds herself feeling anxious and stressed but can't quite put her finger on why. She may have a tendency to suppress her emotions or avoid dealing with them, which leads to more stress and anxiety.

For example, Sarah might have a deadline coming up at work, and instead of acknowledging her stress and finding ways to cope with it, she might distract herself with mindless tasks or ignore her feelings altogether. This can lead to a cycle of stress and avoidance, which can be harmful to her mental health and overall well-being.

By building self-awareness, Sarah can start to recognize when she's feeling stressed or anxious and find healthy ways to cope with those emotions. She can learn to identify her triggers and work to either avoid or manage them. Ultimately, practicing self-awareness can lead to a greater sense of control over her thoughts, emotions, and behaviors, and a more fulfilling life.

Self-awareness is the one thing that separates humans from animals...well, that and the ability to use smartphones. In all seriousness, building self-awareness is crucial on the journey towards self-love. Without it, you might as well be walking through life with your eyes closed and your ears plugged.

Think about it this way: if you don't know yourself, how can you truly love yourself? It's like trying to paint a picture without any paint or a canvas. Building self-awareness allows you to understand your strengths and weaknesses, your likes and dislikes, your passions and fears. It helps you identify your values, your goals, and your purpose in life.

Plus, being self-aware also means that you can identify patterns of behavior that may be holding you back from truly loving yourself. You can recognize negative self-talk and limiting beliefs, and work towards changing them. So, yeah, building self-awareness is kind of a big deal.

So, if you don't have it already, how can you build self-awareness? Let's get into it.

Understanding Your Emotions

To build self-awareness, it's important for women to understand and manage their emotions. Emotions can be tricky, but they are an essential part of being human. You can't just ignore them or stuff them down, because they have a way of coming back up when you least expect it (hello, emotional outbursts in public places!). But don't worry, there are ways to manage them.

One way to understand your emotions is to simply name them. When you're feeling overwhelmed, take a step back and try to identify what you're feeling. Are you sad? Angry? Frustrated? Anxious? Once you can put a name to the emotion, you can start to explore why you're feeling that way. Is there a specific trigger or situation that's causing the emotion? Or is it something deeper, like a core belief or value that's being challenged?

Research shows that naming emotions can have a powerful impact on our mental health. So, the next time you're feeling anxious about an upcoming event, try saying to yourself "I'm feeling anxious" rather than trying to push the feeling away. It may seem small, but it can make a big difference.

Another way to build self-awareness is to practice mindfulness. There it is again! By being mindful of your thoughts, feelings, and bodily sensations, you can develop a better understanding of yourself and your emotions. You can also learn to observe your emotions without being swept away by them, which can be incredibly empowering.

So, to sum it up, building self-awareness is crucial for women who want to cultivate self-love. By understanding and managing our emotions, we can gain a deeper understanding of ourselves and our needs. And by practicing mindfulness, we can learn to observe our thoughts and feelings without judgment, which can be incredibly freeing.

Understanding Your Triggers

So, you're tired of letting your emotions control you like a puppet on a string? Good news, my friend! It's time to understand your triggers and take back the reins! First off, let's talk about what triggers are. They're those things that set you off and make you feel like you're about to explode, whether it's an annoying co-worker or your ex's Instagram page. But fear not, my dear reader, there's hope!

Understanding your triggers can be a powerful tool for building self-awareness and practicing self-love. Triggers are the thoughts, feelings, or situations that can cause a negative emotional reaction. These triggers can be different for everyone and can stem from past experiences or current stressors.

Identifying your triggers can help you become more aware of your emotional responses and can provide insight into why you may react in certain ways. By understanding your triggers, you can also develop strategies to manage your emotions and respond in a more positive and healthy manner.

One way to identify your triggers is to keep a journal of them. Write down any situations or interactions that cause a negative emotional reaction and note the specific emotions you feel. This can help you identify patterns and themes in your triggers.

Another way to understand your triggers is to seek feedback from others. Ask a trusted friend or family member to provide feedback on situations where you may have overreacted or had a strong emotional response. This can help you gain an outside perspective and identify triggers that you may not have recognized on your own.

Finally, it's important to practice self-compassion when identifying your triggers. Recognize that everyone has triggers and it's a natural part of being human. Instead of judging yourself for having triggers, use them as an opportunity for growth and self-improvement.

Research has shown that understanding your triggers can lead to increased emotional regulation and greater psychological well-being (Harvey & Watkins, 2018). By building self-awareness through understanding your triggers, you can take steps towards a more positive and self-loving mindset.

By identifying your triggers, you can learn to manage them better and avoid those emotional landmines. Plus, you'll feel like a badass ninja who can handle anything that comes your way.

Understanding Your Thought Patterns

Understanding your thought patterns is another crucial component of building self-awareness. It involves paying attention to the thoughts that pop into your head and identifying any patterns or recurring themes. For example, do you tend to catastrophize and think of the worst-case scenario in every situation? Do you have a tendency to focus on your flaws and shortcomings instead of your strengths?

Once you start to identify your thought patterns, you can begin to challenge them and reframe them in a more positive and realistic light. This can help you break free from negative self-talk and self-defeating behaviors, bringing you to a sense of zen, always aware of what the evil parts of your brain are trying to do and stopping them in their tracks.

One practical way to understand your thought patterns is to keep a thought journal. Write down any negative or self-critical thoughts that come up throughout the day, and then challenge them with evidence and positive affirmations. This can help you become more aware of your thought patterns and start to rewire your brain for more positive thinking.

But hey, don't just take my word for it! Give it a try and see how it works for you. And remember, be gentle and compassionate with yourself along the way!

Brain Break

Feeling overwhelmed yet? Don't worry; take a deep breath and relax. You don't have to apply all of these strategies at once. In fact, taking things one step at a time is probably the best way to go. You can start by choosing one or two strategies that resonate with you and practice them consistently.

For example, if practicing self-compassion feels like a good fit for you, start by reminding yourself of your positive qualities and saying kind things to yourself when you feel down. Or if mindfulness sounds appealing, try incorporating a short meditation practice into your daily routine.

Remember, building self-awareness and practicing self-love is a journey, not a destination. It's not about being perfect or doing everything right, but rather about showing yourself love and compassion as you work towards your goals. So take it slow, be kind to yourself, and most importantly, have fun with it!

Developing a Growth Mindset

Alright, so you know how sometimes people get stuck in a negative cycle of thinking that they're not good enough, and that their flaws are fixed and unchangeable? You know, what this whole book is basically based on? Well, developing a growth mindset is all about breaking free from that mindset and realizing that you are capable of growth and change. A growth mindset means believing that you can learn, develop, and improve your abilities over time, rather than believing that your talents and skills are predetermined and fixed.

Research has shown that individuals with a growth mindset tend to be more resilient, motivated, and successful in achieving their goals (Dweck, 2006). So, for women who are working on building a foundation for self-love, developing a growth mindset can be a powerful tool to help them overcome obstacles and achieve their goals.

In this section, you're going to get a crash course on how to start developing your own growth mindset. Let's go!

Embracing Change and Challenges

Alright, let's talk about embracing change and challenges, or as we like to call it, "getting out of your comfort zone and into the awkward, uncertain abyss!"

First things first, we have to accept that change is a constant in life. It's going to happen whether we like it or not, so we might as well learn to embrace it. And the best way to do that is to start small. Try something new every day, whether it's trying a new food, taking a different route to work, or talking to a stranger.

Now, when it comes to challenges, we have to remind ourselves that they are opportunities for growth and learning. Instead of running away from them, we need to lean into them with open arms and a curious mind. And if we fail, that's okay! Failure is not the end of the world; it's just a learning opportunity.

So, the next time you're faced with a challenge or a change, take a deep breath, channel your inner superhero, and go for it! Remember, you're stronger and more capable than you think.

Emphasizing Effort

Now, it's important to understand that putting in effort is crucial for achieving your goals and developing a growth mindset. The belief that natural ability alone can guarantee success is just a myth.

Research shows that individuals who believe in the power of effort and persistence are more likely to achieve their goals and experience personal growth (Dweck, 2006). It's not about being born with a certain set of skills or talents, but rather about the effort you put in to develop those skills.

So, how can you emphasize effort over natural ability in your own life? First, start by recognizing the value of hard work and perseverance. Instead of giving up when faced with a challenge, push through and keep working at it. Celebrate your progress and the effort you put in, rather than just focusing on the end result.

In short, remember that effort and perseverance are the keys to success and personal growth. So keep pushing yourself, embrace challenges, and don't be afraid to learn and grow from your mistakes.

Cultivate a Love of Learning

Now, I know what you might be thinking: "Learning? That sounds like school. I already graduated; why do I need to keep learning?" But hold on there, champ. Learning doesn't just happen in a classroom. It can happen anywhere, anytime. And when you have a love of learning, it can help you grow as a person and boost your self-confidence.

So, how can you cultivate a love of learning? Well, first of all, start with your interests. What are you passionate about? What topics or activities make you feel energized and excited? Maybe it's cooking, or painting, or hiking, or astronomy. Whatever it is, start diving deeper into those areas. Read books, watch videos, take classes, join groups, attend events. The more you learn about something you love, the more you'll want to learn.

Try to make learning a daily habit. Even if it's just something small, like listening to a podcast or reading an article during your commute or watching a tutorial on YouTube while you cook dinner. When you make learning a part of your daily routine, it becomes easier and more natural.

Research shows that a love of learning is strongly linked to personal growth and well-being (Buchanan & Bardi, 2010). So go ahead and dive into that new topic or activity that's been on your mind. Who knows? It might just lead to a whole new passion and a greater love for yourself.

Reframe Your Failure as Feedback

So, you tried something and it didn't work out. Maybe you fell flat on your face or maybe you just didn't get the result you were hoping for. It happens to the best of us! But instead of beating yourself up over it, why not reframe failure as feedback?

Here's the deal: Failure is not the end of the world. In fact, it's often just the beginning of a valuable learning experience. When things don't go as planned, it's an opportunity to reflect on what went wrong, what you could do better next time, and how you can grow from the experience.

For women trying to build a foundation for self-love, reframing failure as feedback is especially important. It helps to shift the focus from self-blame to self-improvement, and it encourages a growth mindset. Plus, when you learn to embrace failure as a natural part of the learning process, you'll be more willing to take risks and try new things - which can lead to some pretty amazing results!

So, how can you start reframing failure as feedback? Here are a few tips:

1. Take a step back and reflect on what happened. What went wrong? What could you have done differently? What did you learn from the experience?
2. Reframe your self-talk. Instead of saying things like "I'm such a failure" or "I'll never be good at this", try saying things like "I'm still learning" or "This is just feedback for next time."
3. Focus on the positive. Even if things didn't go as planned, there's usually something positive to take away from the experience. Maybe you made progress in a certain area, or you gained valuable insights into what doesn't work.
4. Keep going. Don't let failure hold you back. Use the feedback you've gained to keep pushing forward and trying new things. After all, the only real failure is giving up!

Remember, reframing failure as feedback takes practice. But the more you do it, the easier it becomes. So, the next time things don't go as planned, take a deep breath, dust yourself off, and remember, failure is just feedback in disguise!

Surround Yourself with Growth-Minded People

We've talked about various ways to cultivate a growth mindset, but one surefire method is to surround yourself with positive influences. Are you starting to see a theme yet? Positivity is key. That means surrounding yourself with people who are supportive, encouraging, and who inspire you to be your best self. It also means exposing yourself to positive media, books, podcasts, and anything else that inspires you to grow and learn.

But here's the thing: it's not just about surrounding yourself with positivity; it's also about actively seeking it out. Seek out mentors, coaches, and role models who can guide you on your journey to personal growth. Attend workshops, conferences, and events that challenge you to learn new things and meet new people.

When it comes to media consumption, be mindful of what you're exposing yourself to. Instead of scrolling mindlessly through social media, choose to follow accounts that inspire you and share valuable insights. Listen to podcasts and read books that teach you new skills and challenge your thinking.

By actively seeking out positive influences, you're setting yourself up for success. You're surrounding yourself with a community of people who believe in you, support you, and challenge you to be your best self. And with this kind of support, you can overcome any obstacle and achieve anything you set your mind to.

Alright, now that we've covered ways to develop a growth mindset, let's shift our focus to celebrating small victories. Because when it comes to building self-love, it's not just about the big accomplishments; it's also about the small steps we take along the way. So, let's take a moment to recognize and celebrate the progress we've made so far and continue to move forward with a growth mindset; see, you're already putting it to practice!

Celebrating Small Victories

So, we've talked about developing a growth mindset as a way to build a foundation for self-love. But here's the thing: sometimes, when we're in the midst of our self-love journey, it can feel like we're not making progress at all. We might set big goals for ourselves, and when we don't achieve them right away, it can be discouraging. That's where celebrating small victories comes in.

See, celebrating the little things can help us stay motivated and keep us on track. When we recognize and acknowledge the progress we're making, even if it's just a small step, it can give us the boost we need to keep going.

Building Self-Esteem Through Accomplishments

There's another facet of self-love: self-esteem. Building self-esteem through accomplishments is an important aspect of celebrating small victories. When we achieve something we've been working towards, it can give us a sense of pride and self-worth. According to a study by Baumeister et al. (2003), individuals with high self-esteem tend to view themselves positively and see themselves as capable of achieving their goals, while individuals with low self-esteem may feel powerless and incapable of achieving success.

To build self-esteem through accomplishments, you can start by setting achievable goals for yourself. It's important to make these goals specific, measurable, and time-bound. For example, if you want to improve your physical fitness, you can set a goal of going to the gym three times a week for the next month.

Take some time and think of a small goal you can set for yourself, something that you can achieve in the next month. Maybe it's reading a new book (like this one; good job, you're already reaching your goals!), or trying a new hobby. Either way, write it down and give yourself a time-limit to do it.

Once you achieve a goal, you should take the time to acknowledge your accomplishments and feel proud of yourself; you did a good thing! Take yourself out to dinner girl! You can also use the accomplishment as motivation to set and achieve new goals.

It's worth noting that building self-esteem through accomplishments should not be your only source of self-worth. It's important for you to also recognize your inherent worth as a human being, separate from your achievements. Remember, self-esteem and self-worth are two totally different things.

Conclusion

Congratulations on building a solid foundation for self-love! But our journey doesn't end here. To
continue nurturing your relationship with yourself, it's time to dive into the next chapter: Cultivating Self-Compassion and Self-Care.

In this chapter, we'll explore the transformative power of self-compassion and the importance of taking care of yourself. We'll discover how practicing self-compassion can bring kindness and understanding to your inner dialogue, and how self-care can be a powerful act of self-love.

So, what's the call to action? Well, it's simple:

Grab a cozy blanket, make yourself a cup of your favorite beverage, and settle into a comfortable spot. Open the next chapter with an open mind and an open heart, ready to embrace self-compassion and self-care. Prepare to learn practical strategies and techniques to cultivate self-compassion and incorporate self-care practices into your daily life. Remember, this journey is all about progress, not perfection. Be patient and gentle with yourself as you explore these concepts and begin implementing them. Most importantly, believe in yourself and your capacity for self-love. You deserve love, care, and compassion.

So, my friend, let's embark on the next chapter together. Get ready to cultivate self-compassion and self-care, and watch as your relationship with yourself blossoms into something truly beautiful.

Are you ready? Let's do this!

Takeaways

- Realizing your worth comes from a constant appreciation of your own unique talents and achievements.
- Challenging limiting beliefs and negative self-talk are crucial to journeying towards self-love.
- Self-love comes with self-awareness. Understanding your emotions, triggers, and thought patterns are three ways you can become more self-aware.
- Developing a growth mindset is important for self-love. It involves recognizing failure as an opportunity to improve.
- Celebrating small victories is just as important as celebrating large ones to motivate you towards a better life.

CHAPTER 3

CULTIVATING SELF-COMPASSION AND SELF-CARE

"Self-compassion is simply giving the same kindness to ourselves that we would give to others." - Christopher Germer

Self-compassion is about nurturing a gentle and supportive relationship with ourselves, acknowledging our imperfections and struggles without judgment, and embracing our inherent worthiness of love and care. It serves as a powerful reminder to be our own best friend and ally on our journey toward self-love.

Self-compassion and self-care are two essential ingredients in the recipe for self-love. By learning to treat ourselves with kindness and prioritize our well-being, we can build a solid foundation for a fulfilling and joyful life.

In this chapter, we will explore the significance and benefits of self-compassion, as well as practical techniques for practicing mindfulness, loving-kindness, and self-forgiveness. We will also delve into the different types of self-care, from physical and emotional to mental and spiritual, and provide tips for incorporating self-care into your daily routine. By creating a supportive environment and nurturing positive relationships, you can cultivate a deep sense of self-love and inner peace.

Understanding Self-Compassion

Self-compassion is the art of giving ourselves a big ol' bear hug of kindness and understanding. It's like having a personal cheerleader who reminds us that we're human and deserving of love, even when we stumble and fall (figuratively, of course). Let's dive into what self-compassion is all about and why it's worth embracing with open arms.

What is self-compassion, you ask? Well, my friend, self-compassion is like having a warm cup of hot cocoa on a chilly winter's day for your soul. It involves treating ourselves with kindness, understanding, and acceptance, especially in moments when we're feeling vulnerable, imperfect, or weighed down by difficult challenges. It's about being a friend to ourselves, offering empathy, and letting go of harsh self-criticism. Who doesn't want a friend like that?

Now, I know you're wondering, "Is there any science to back up this self-compassion stuff?" You betcha! Research shows that self-compassion is linked to increased psychological well-being, reduced levels of stress, anxiety, and depression, and greater resilience in the face of adversity. So, it's not just some woo-woo concept; it's backed by scientific goodness.

Now let's get specific about the benefits. Self-compassion isn't just a warm and fuzzy feeling; it brings some serious benefits to the table. For starters, it helps us navigate life's challenges with greater resilience. When we embrace self-compassion, we're less likely to beat ourselves up over mistakes or setbacks. Instead, we bounce back quicker, learn from our experiences, and grow stronger.

You know that pesky inner critic we all have? The one who loves to rain on our parade and tell us we're not good enough? Well, self-compassion helps us put that critic in its place. It allows us to cultivate a kinder, more supportive inner voice that celebrates our efforts and acknowledges our worthiness. So long, inner critic—no more room for you in this self-compassion party!

Self-compassion also helps us develop a healthier relationship with ourselves. It encourages us to embrace our flaws, acknowledge our humanity, and treat ourselves with the same compassion we extend to others. By nurturing self-compassion, we create a loving and nurturing environment within ourselves that promotes emotional well-being and a greater sense of self-love.

Techniques for Practicing Self-Compassion

Now that we've wrapped our minds around the power of self-compassion, it's time to roll up our sleeves and put it into action. Get ready to shower yourself with some serious love and care. In this section, we'll explore practical techniques to cultivate self-compassion and nourish our souls. Get ready for some self-love boot camp!

Loving-Kindness

Imagine wrapping yourself in a cozy blanket of self-kindness. Start by speaking to yourself with the same warmth and gentleness you'd offer a dear friend. When that inner critic starts yapping, respond with words of comfort and understanding. "It's okay, darling. We all make mistakes. You're doing the best you can, and that's more than enough." Ah, doesn't that feel like a warm hug for the soul?

Also known as Metta in the Buddhist tradition, loving-kindness is an ancient, powerful practice that involves cultivating unconditional love, compassion, and goodwill towards yourself and others. As you use this practice, you develop a deep sense of kindness, empathy, and genuine care for yourself and all beings.

In the context of self-compassion, loving-kindness is about extending that same warmth, understanding, and love to ourselves that we would naturally offer to others. Loving-kindness involves intentionally generating and directing positive thoughts, wishes, and intentions towards yourself. It may include repeating phrases or affirmations such as "May I be happy. May I be healthy. May I be at peace." By actively engaging in this practice, we develop a nurturing and loving relationship with ourselves, fostering a deep sense of self-acceptance and self-care.

It's important to note that loving-kindness is not about self-indulgence or selfishness. Instead, it encourages us to cultivate a genuine and unconditional love for ourselves, recognizing our inherent worthiness and embracing our imperfections. Through loving-kindness, we can heal emotional wounds, soften self-judgment, and create a nurturing foundation for self-love to flourish.

So, my friend, let's sprinkle some loving-kindness into our lives, showering ourselves with the sweet nectar of compassion, and watch as our hearts blossom with love and kindness. May we all embrace this practice and cultivate a deep reservoir of self-love that radiates outwards, touching the lives of those around us.

Self-Forgiveness and Embracing Imperfections

Repeat after me: "I am beautifully imperfect, and that's what makes me unique." Embrace your flaws and quirks because they're what make you, well, you! Instead of striving for unattainable perfection, celebrate your progress, growth, and the beauty in your imperfections. So what if you burnt that batch of cookies? At least you tried, and next time, they'll be even more delicious (hopefully).

Self-forgiveness is an essential component of self-compassion, as it involves extending understanding, empathy, and forgiveness to ourselves for our past mistakes, shortcomings, and perceived failures.

Self-forgiveness comes from a place of recognizing our own humanity and embracing our imperfections. We're all beautifully flawed creatures on this wild journey called life, and we're bound to stumble and make mistakes along the way. It's about accepting that we're not perfect and that we're allowed to be flawed; haven't you ever heard that Hannah Montana song?

When we practice self-compassion, it's like opening a door to self-forgiveness. We acknowledge that we're not defined by our mistakes or regrets, but rather by our capacity to learn, grow, and evolve. It's about releasing the burden of self-blame, guilt, and shame, and embracing a mindset of self-acceptance and self-love.

Self-forgiveness doesn't mean brushing off our actions or pretending they didn't happen. It's about acknowledging the pain or hurt we may have caused ourselves or others, taking responsibility for our actions, and committing to making amends and learning from those experiences. It's a process of healing, allowing ourselves to move forward with compassion and understanding.

Here are some practical ways you can dive into this transformative practice:

1. Write a self-forgiveness letter: Grab a pen and paper, or open a blank document, and write a heartfelt letter of self-forgiveness. Pour out your emotions, acknowledging the pain or disappointment caused by your actions. Express your sincere apology to yourself, and emphasize your commitment to growth, self-improvement, and self-love.

2. Practice mindfulness and self-compassion meditation: Set aside a few moments each day to engage in mindfulness and self-compassion meditation. Allow yourself to sit with your thoughts and emotions, observing them without judgment. Cultivate self-compassion by offering yourself kind and comforting words during your practice.

3. Seek support and guidance: Don't be afraid to reach out to supportive friends, family members, or even professionals like

therapists or counselors. Sharing your experiences and emotions with others can provide valuable perspective and support as you navigate the path of self-forgiveness.

So, my friend, let's give ourselves permission to let go of past mistakes and embrace the healing power of self-forgiveness. Let's offer ourselves the same forgiveness and understanding we would extend to a dear friend or loved one. Remember, we're all a work in progress, and it's through self-forgiveness that we create space for growth, transformation, and ultimately, a more loving and compassionate relationship with ourselves.

The Compassionate Pause

When faced with a challenging situation or a bout of self-criticism, take a compassionate pause. Step back and ask yourself, "What would I say to a friend going through this? How can I offer myself the same understanding and encouragement?" Give yourself the gift of perspective and respond with kindness, just as you would to someone you care about.

The compassionate pause is all about giving yourself permission to pause, breathe, and respond to difficult situations with kindness and understanding. It's a moment of intentional awareness where you take a step back from your immediate reactions and allow space for self-compassion to arise.

Here's how you can practice the compassionate pause:

1. Recognize the trigger: Become aware of situations or events that typically trigger negative emotions or self-criticism. It could be a

mistake, a failure, a criticism from others, or even a challenging interaction. Acknowledge the trigger and its impact on your emotional well-being.

2. Pause and take a breath: In the midst of the trigger, pause for a moment and take a deep breath. This simple act helps create a gap between the trigger and your response. Allow yourself to be fully present in the moment, letting go of any immediate reactions or judgments.

3. Offer self-compassion: Once you've taken that pause, bring self-compassion into the picture. Remind yourself that everyone makes mistakes, faces challenges, and experiences setbacks. Offer yourself words of kindness, understanding, and support. You might say something like, "It's okay, everyone makes mistakes. I am doing my best, and I deserve kindness and understanding."

4. Shift the perspective: During the compassionate pause, challenge any negative self-talk or self-judgment that may arise. Ask yourself if there's another perspective or a more compassionate way to view the situation. Consider what you would say to a friend in a similar situation and extend that same compassion to yourself.

5. Choose a compassionate response: After offering yourself self-compassion and gaining a fresh perspective, choose a response that aligns with your values and promotes your well-being. It might involve setting boundaries, expressing your needs assertively, or simply giving yourself permission to let go of unrealistic expectations.

The compassionate pause allows you to break free from habitual reactions and cultivate a kinder and more self-compassionate approach to life's challenges. It empowers you to respond to difficult situations with grace and understanding, nurturing a deeper sense of self-love and well-being. The compassionate pause is an extremely important step in one of the biggest aspects of self-compassion: mindfulness.

Mindfulness

Ah, mindfulness—the art of being fully present in the moment, non-judgmentally. It's a wonderful tool for cultivating self-compassion. Let's dive into how mindfulness can nourish your self-compassion practice.

Mindfulness is all about bringing your attention to the present moment, without judgment or attachment. It allows you to observe your thoughts, emotions, and sensations with curiosity and acceptance. By practicing mindfulness, you develop a greater awareness of your inner experiences and cultivate a kind and non-reactive attitude towards yourself.

Mindfulness helps you become aware of your thoughts, emotions, and bodily sensations in the present moment. It allows you to notice self-critical or judgmental thoughts and gently redirect your attention to the present. This space allows you to respond to yourself with compassion and kindness, recognizing that your thoughts and emotions are natural and impermanent.

Mindfulness helps you tune in to your own needs and well-being. It allows you to notice when you're feeling stressed, overwhelmed, or in need of self-care. By being present with yourself, you can make intentional choices to prioritize self-care and engage in activities that nourish your body, mind, and soul.

As you practice mindfulness, you cultivate a gentle and kind attitude towards yourself. Instead of harsh self-criticism, you learn to respond to your experiences with understanding. This kind and supportive inner dialogue promotes self-compassion and fosters a sense of well-being.

Incorporating mindfulness into your daily life can support your self-compassion practice by fostering self-awareness, acceptance, and kindness. Whether it's through formal meditation practices, mindful breathing exercises, or simply bringing mindful awareness to everyday activities, mindfulness offers a powerful gateway to self-compassion. But how can you do it yourself?

Let's explore some practical ways you can incorporate mindfulness into your daily life to enhance your self-compassion practice.

1. Mindful Breathing: Take a few moments throughout the day to focus on your breath. Close your eyes, bring your attention to your breath, and simply observe the sensation of each inhale and exhale. If your mind wanders, gently bring your focus back to your breath. This simple practice can help ground you in the present moment and create a sense of calm and self-awareness.

2. Body Scan Meditation: Set aside some time to do a body scan meditation. Start from the top of your head and slowly move down through each part of your body, noticing any sensations, tensions, or areas of discomfort. As you become aware of these sensations, offer yourself compassion and kindness. Imagine sending love and acceptance to each part of your body, embracing it just as it is.

3. Mindful Eating: Pay attention to the experience of eating. Slow down, savor each bite, and fully engage your senses. Notice the

colors, textures, and flavors of the food. Be present with each moment as you nourish your body. Cultivate gratitude for the nourishment and pleasure that food brings to your life.

4. Everyday Mindfulness: Infuse mindfulness into your daily activities. Whether it's brushing your teeth, taking a shower, or washing dishes, bring your full attention to the task at hand. Notice the sensations, smells, and sounds associated with the activity. By bringing mindfulness into these ordinary moments, you can cultivate a greater sense of presence and self-compassion throughout the day.

5. Loving-Kindness Meditation: You know this one! Practice a loving-kindness meditation to cultivate compassion for yourself and others. Sit comfortably, close your eyes, and repeat phrases of kindness and well-being. Start by offering loving-kindness to yourself, then extend it to loved ones, acquaintances, and even challenging individuals. This practice can foster a sense of connection, empathy, and self-compassion.

6. Mindful Movement: Engage in mindful movement practices such as yoga, tai chi, or walking meditation. As you move your body, pay attention to the sensations, the breath, and the connection between mind and body. Allow movement to become a form of meditation, bringing a sense of peace, joy, and self-compassion.

Remember, my friend, that mindfulness is a journey, and it's all about bringing gentle awareness and kindness to the present moment. Experiment with these practices, find what resonates with you, and make mindfulness a part of your daily life. You don't have to do *everything* on this list; it's just to provide some options for you to try out.

It's through these small moments of mindfulness that you can nurture self-compassion and create a more loving relationship with yourself. So, take a deep breath, be present, and let mindfulness be your compass on this beautiful path of self-compassion and self-care.

Exploring Different Types of Self-Care

Get ready to explore the wonderful world of self-care, my friend. In this section, we're going to dive into the different types of self-care: physical, emotional, mental, and spiritual. Each type plays a unique role in nurturing your well-being and practicing self-love. So, let's put on our self-care hats and embark on this adventure together!

Physical Self-Care

Let's give your body some love! Physical self-care involves taking care of your physical health and vitality. It includes activities like regular exercise, getting enough sleep, nourishing your body with nutritious food, staying hydrated, and tending to your physical well-being.

Physical self-care is all about taking care of your body, treating it like the magnificent temple it is. Not only does it make you feel good, but it also has a plethora of benefits that will leave you strutting around like a confident peacock. So, let's break it down and discover why physical self-care is worth all of the sweaty effort!

The first positive thing that physical self-care is going to impact is your energy levels. Engaging in physical activities, whether it's dancing, jogging, or doing yoga poses, can revitalize your body and pump up those energy levels. Say goodbye to feeling sluggish and hello to an energized and vibrant you!

Secondly, exercise and physical movement release endorphins, those lovely little neurotransmitters that make you feel oh-so-good. They act as natural mood boosters and can help alleviate stress, anxiety, and even symptoms of depression. So get that body moving and unleash your inner happiness ninja!

Thirdly, when you make physical self-care a priority, you're doing your body a huge favor. Regular exercise helps improve cardiovascular health, strengthen muscles and bones, and enhance overall physical fitness. It's like giving your body a tune-up, making sure everything runs smoothly and efficiently.

Fourth, the sweet embrace of a good night's sleep! Physical self-care can contribute to a better quality of sleep. Regular exercise helps regulate your sleep patterns, making it easier to fall asleep and wake up feeling refreshed. So you can bid farewell to tossing and turning and say hello to blissful slumber.

Fifth, taking care of your physical health can boost your self-esteem and body confidence. Engaging in activities that make you feel strong, flexible, and empowered can help you embrace and appreciate your body just as it is. Loving yourself from head to toe? That's what it's all about!

Finally, when life throws those stress grenades at you, physical self-care is like a shield of resilience. Engaging in exercise or physical activities helps reduce stress hormones like cortisol and releases tension from your body.

It's like a mini-vacation for your mind and body, allowing you to find your inner zen.

So, my fabulous friend, let physical self-care be your secret weapon in the quest for self-love. Embrace the joy of movement, find activities that bring you pleasure, and revel in the amazing benefits that come with it. Whether it's dancing like nobody's watching, going for a scenic hike, or practicing some fancy yoga poses, prioritize your physical well-being and bask in the wonderful effects it will have on your overall self-love journey.

Emotional Self-Care

Ah, emotions, those rollercoasters of life! Emotional self-care involves tending to your emotional well-being and nurturing your feelings. It's about acknowledging and validating your emotions, expressing yourself authentically, and creating healthy emotional boundaries. Find activities that bring you joy, such as journaling, talking to a supportive friend, practicing mindfulness, or engaging in creative outlets like painting or playing music.

Emotional self-care, my friend, is all about nurturing and tending to your precious emotional well-being. It's like giving your heart a big warm hug and saying, "Hey, emotions, I've got your back!" So, let's dive into the benefits of emotional self-care.

Probably unsurprisingly, emotional self-care helps you build resilience and cope with life's ups and downs more effectively. It allows you to process your emotions, express them in healthy ways, and find inner balance and peace. It's like having an emotional superhero cape that helps you navigate the rollercoaster of life with grace and strength.

Emotional self-care also contributes to self-awareness, something that's important in self-love. When you prioritize emotional self-care, you become more attuned to your own emotions, thoughts, and needs. You develop a deeper understanding of yourself, your triggers, and your patterns. This self-awareness is like having a superpower that empowers you to make conscious choices and respond to situations in a way that aligns with your authentic self.

In even greater news, emotional self-care allows you to show up more fully in your relationships. When you take care of your emotional well-being, you become more present, empathetic, and compassionate towards yourself and others. It helps you communicate effectively, set boundaries, and foster deeper connections. It's like sprinkling love and kindness onto your relationships, creating a beautiful bond.

Emotional self-care works similarly to physical self-care; when life throws its challenges your way, emotional self-care becomes your shield against stress. Engaging in activities that bring you joy, practicing relaxation techniques, and expressing your emotions can help reduce stress levels and promote a sense of calm. It's like having your own personal stress-busting toolkit that you can whip out whenever life gets a little too chaotic.

Finally, emotional self-care builds your emotional resilience muscle. It equips you with the skills to bounce back from setbacks, navigate difficult emotions, and find the strength to keep going. It's like having a secret power-up that empowers you to rise above challenges and come out even stronger on the other side.

Embrace the beautiful messiness of your emotions, give yourself permission to feel deeply, and know that you are worthy of emotional care. Let your emotional self-care be a nurturing sanctuary that supports and uplifts you on your journey towards self-love. You've got this!

Mental Self-Care

Time to give your marvelous mind some tender loving care! Mental self-care involves nurturing your mental well-being and cognitive processes. It means taking time to rest your mind, engage in activities that stimulate your intellect, and cultivate a positive mindset. You can try activities like reading, solving puzzles, learning something new, practicing meditation, or engaging in positive affirmations to foster mental well-being.

So, why is mental self-care important for self-love? Let me enlighten you:

Just like your body needs nutritious food, your mind craves mental nourishment. Engaging in activities that stimulate your intellect, such as reading, learning new things, solving puzzles, or engaging in creative pursuits, feeds your mind and keeps it sharp and vibrant.

Secondly, taking care of your mental well-being can boost your self-esteem and confidence. When you challenge yourself mentally and accomplish new things, you build a sense of competence and achievement. Each step forward in your mental growth enhances your belief in your own abilities and worth.

Like the other types of self-care, mental self-care practices, like relaxation techniques, meditation, or mindfulness exercises, can help alleviate stress and anxiety. By calming the mind and cultivating a sense of inner peace, you create a sanctuary within yourself, free from the tumultuous storms of worries and negative thoughts. Now we're at triple stress-relief!

Furthermore, engaging in activities that stimulate your brain, such as puzzles, brain teasers, or learning new skills, can improve cognitive function. It enhances memory, focus, problem-solving abilities, and creativity, empowering you to navigate life's challenges with clarity and agility.

Fourth, mental self-care involves nurturing positive thoughts and cultivating a healthy mindset. By challenging negative self-talk, practicing gratitude, and reframing negative situations, you cultivate a positive perspective that fuels self-love and encourages a compassionate and optimistic outlook on life.

Finally, mental and emotional well-being go hand in hand. Engaging in activities that promote mental wellness, such as therapy, journaling, or engaging in hobbies, can help you process emotions, gain clarity, and develop healthy coping mechanisms. A balanced and nurtured mind lays the foundation for emotional resilience and well-being.

So, my wondrous friend, prioritizing mental self-care is like giving your mind a big, warm hug. It's about honoring your intellectual needs, nourishing your thoughts, and embracing the beauty of your own mind. Remember, your mind is a marvelous creation, capable of growth, learning, and endless possibilities. Treat it with kindness, feed it with knowledge, and watch it flourish with self-love. Embrace the wonders of mental self-care and unleash the infinite power of your mind!

Spiritual Self-Care

Feed your soul, my friend! Spiritual self-care is about nurturing your connection to something greater than yourself and finding meaning and purpose in life. It can involve engaging in practices like meditation, prayer, spending time in nature, practicing gratitude, or exploring your beliefs and values. Discover what brings you a sense of peace, awe, and transcendence, and weave it into your daily life.

Ah, the ethereal realm of spiritual self-care awaits! Let's embark on a whimsical exploration of this sacred domain and explore the benefits it holds for your soul.

Spiritual self-care invites you to tap into your inner wisdom, intuition, and the deeper aspects of your being. It's a journey of self-discovery, allowing you to explore your values, purpose, and meaning in life. By connecting with your inner self, you can navigate the world with greater clarity and authenticity.

Secondly, engaging in spiritual practices fosters a sense of peace and serenity amidst life's chaotic dance. Whether through meditation, prayer, mindfulness, or nature walks, these practices help you find solace, stillness, and a refuge from the demands of daily life. They offer a gentle reminder to slow down, breathe, and reconnect with your inner calm.

Third, spiritual self-care often emphasizes compassion and love for oneself and others. It encourages acts of kindness, forgiveness, and cultivating a heart-centered approach to life. By nurturing your spiritual side, you can deepen your capacity for empathy, compassion, and understanding.

Fourth, spiritual self-care can strengthen your inner resilience and fortify your spirit in the face of life's challenges. It provides a source of strength and support during difficult times, helping you navigate adversity with grace and courage.

Finally, spiritual self-care can involve connecting with like-minded individuals or joining spiritual communities that share your beliefs and values. This sense of community provides a supportive network where you can deepen your spiritual practices, engage in meaningful discussions, and share your journey with others.

Remember, self-care isn't about ticking off boxes or following a rigid checklist. It's about creating a personalized self-care routine that honors and supports your unique needs and desires. Embrace the adventure of discovering which self-care activities resonate with you the most in each of these areas.

So, my dear friend, let's venture forth into the world of physical, emotional, mental, and spiritual self-care. Explore, experiment, and be open to finding your own unique blend of self-care practices that will nurture your mind, body, and soul. You deserve it, and together, we'll cultivate a beautiful self-care routine that nourishes your self-love journey.

Incorporating Self-Care into Daily Routines

So you know what you need to do, but how? It's hard to think of everything you should do, like self-care, instead of all the things you're already overwhelmed with doing, but trust me, after a bit of practice, self-care won't feel even a little bit like a chore. Let's get into the different techniques you can incorporate into your routine to start practicing the different types of self-care.

Tips for Physical Self-Care

Time to get those self-care gears in motion and start implementing physical self-care into your fabulous life. Here are some practical steps to get you started:

1. Find Activities You Enjoy: The key to sticking with physical self-care is finding activities that you genuinely enjoy and starting small. Whether it's dancing, swimming, hiking, playing a sport, or even just taking leisurely walks in nature, choose activities that make your heart sing and your body dance with joy. Make it a fun and enjoyable experience!

2. Schedule It in Your Calendar: Treat your physical self-care as a non-negotiable appointment with yourself. Block out dedicated time in your calendar for your chosen activities. Treat it as seriously as you would a doctor's appointment or an important meeting. By scheduling it, you prioritize it and make it a priority in your life.

3. Make It Social: Physical self-care doesn't have to be a solitary affair. Invite friends, family, or loved ones to join you in your chosen activities. It can be a great way to bond, have fun, and motivate each other. Plus, sharing laughter and sweating together adds an extra dose of awesomeness to the experience.

4. Celebrate Your Achievements: Celebrate even the smallest victories along your physical self-care journey. Did you go for a walk today? Awesome! Did you try a new exercise class? Fantastic!

Celebrate these achievements, pat yourself on the back, and acknowledge the progress you're making. You deserve it!

Remember, my friend, physical self-care is about nourishing and honoring your body. It's not about punishment or unrealistic expectations. Be kind to yourself, enjoy the process, and embrace the joy that comes with taking care of your physical well-being. You've got this, and your body will thank you for it!

Tips for Emotional Self-Care

You deserve to cultivate a rich emotional landscape where joy, love, sadness, and everything in between can coexist harmoniously. So, take a deep breath, tune in to your emotions, and let's embark on this beautiful journey of emotional self-care together. Your heart will thank you, and your emotional well-being will flourish like never before.

Here are some practical ways you can start practicing emotional self-care in your daily life:

1. Check-in with Yourself: Take a few moments each day to pause and check in with yourself. Ask yourself how you're feeling emotionally and honor those emotions without judgment. This simple act of self-awareness can help you better understand your needs and emotions.

2. Express Yourself: Find healthy ways to express your emotions. Write in a journal, create art, talk to a trusted friend, or engage in activities that allow you to process and release your emotions. Don't shy away from experiencing and expressing your feelings; they are a natural and essential part of being human.

3. Engage in Activities that Bring Joy: Identify activities that uplift your spirits and bring you joy. It could be anything from taking a walk in nature, dancing to your favorite music, practicing a hobby, or spending time with loved ones. Make time for these activities regularly to nurture your emotional well-being.

4. Practice Emotional Resilience: Embrace challenges and setbacks as opportunities for growth. Cultivate a mindset that views failures as learning experiences and allows you to bounce back stronger. Develop coping strategies and resilience-building practices that help you navigate difficult emotions and situations.

Remember, my dear friend, emotional self-care is an ongoing journey. It's about making conscious choices every day to prioritize your emotional well-being, honor your emotions, and tend to your heart with love and compassion.

Tips for Mental Self-Care

So, my eager explorer of the mind, let's delve into the realm of practical mental self-care! Here are some delightful ways you can cultivate a nourishing mental oasis:

1. Feed Your Curiosity: Expand your knowledge and stimulate your intellect by reading books, exploring new topics of interest, or taking up a new hobby. Nourish your inquisitive mind and let your curiosity roam free, for it is the gateway to endless discoveries.

2. Disconnect and Unplug: Take regular breaks from technology and the digital world. Disconnect from the constant barrage of notifications and immerse yourself in activities that nourish your

soul, such as spending time in nature, enjoying quality time with loved ones, or simply indulging in moments of solitude.

3. Prioritize Rest and Sleep: Give your mind the rest it craves by prioritizing quality sleep and relaxation. Create a soothing bedtime routine, practice good sleep hygiene, and listen to your body's cues for rest. A well-rested mind is a refreshed and rejuvenated mind.

4. Engage in Brain-Boosting Activities: Challenge your mind with brain-boosting activities like puzzles, crosswords, or learning a new language. Engaging in activities that stimulate your cognitive abilities keeps your mind sharp and vibrant.

Embrace the practices that resonate with you, make them a delightful part of your routine, and watch your mental garden blossom with self-compassion and love. Your mind is a treasure trove waiting to be nurtured, so embark on this adventure of mental self-care and unlock the infinite possibilities that lie within you!

Tips for Spiritual Self-Care

Ah, the integration of spiritual self-care into your daily routine is a delightful endeavor! Here are some whimsical and practical ways to infuse your days with spiritual essence:

1. Morning Rituals: Begin your day with intention by creating a sacred morning ritual. It can include practices like meditation, prayer, journaling, or reading spiritual texts. Set aside a few

moments to connect with your inner self, express gratitude, and set positive intentions for the day ahead.

2. Nature Communion: Connect with the natural world as a spiritual practice. Take leisurely walks in parks or gardens, letting the sights, sounds, and scents awaken your senses. Engage in grounding activities like gardening or simply sitting under a tree, allowing nature's wisdom to nourish your spirit.

3. Rituals and Ceremonies: Embrace rituals and ceremonies that hold significance for you. It can be lighting candles, burning incense, or performing rituals aligned with your spiritual path. These rituals can be performed daily, on special occasions, or during transitional periods to mark and honor the sacredness of life.

4. Connection and Community: Seek connections with like-minded individuals who share your spiritual interests. Attend spiritual gatherings, workshops, or join online communities where you can engage in meaningful discussions, share experiences, and learn from one another's journeys.

Remember, dear seeker of spiritual solace, the essence of spiritual self-care lies in infusing your daily life with intention, presence, and reverence. Let your heart be your guide as you weave these practices into your routine, nurturing your spiritual well-being and deepening your connection to the sacred. Embrace the magic that unfolds when you cultivate your spiritual self-care, and may your journey be filled with illumination and divine grace!

Creating a Supportive Environment

Picture this: a space that embraces your self-care rituals with open arms, where tranquility and serenity reside, and where your well-being takes center stage. Such an environment plays a crucial role in nurturing your self-love journey. Here's why:

A supportive environment creates a nurturing sanctuary for your self-care practices. It's a space where you can escape the demands of the outside world and immerse yourself in self-nurturing activities. It helps minimize distractions, free you from the buzzing of electronic devices, interruptions, or outside noise. By creating a peaceful ambiance, you can immerse yourself in the present moment and give your self-care practices the attention they deserve.

Creating a supportive environment allows you to establish boundaries and ensure privacy. It's a space where you can freely express yourself, explore your emotions, and engage in practices without the fear of judgment or interruption. Having this sense of privacy fosters a safe and comfortable space for deep introspection and self-discovery.

Remember, your environment has the power to either uplift or hinder your self-love journey. By intentionally creating a supportive environment for yourself, you invite an atmosphere that encourages and embraces your self-care rituals. So, embrace the art of curating a supportive environment and let it become a harmonious cocoon that nurtures your soul and amplifies your self-love journey.

Setting Up a Physical Space

Let me guide you through this delightful process with a touch of whimsy and practicality. Here's how you can create a space that resonates with your self-care needs:

Start by finding a designated area in your home that can be your sacred spot for self-care. It could be a cozy nook, a corner of your bedroom, or even a dedicated room if you have the luxury. Select a space that feels comfortable, peaceful, and aligned with your personal style and preferences.

Before transforming your space, declutter and organize it. Clear away any unnecessary items, ensuring a clean and serene environment. This will allow for a fresh start and provide a blank canvas for your self-care sanctuary.

Transforming your space would involve designing and incorporating things into your space that make you feel calm and cared for. Tailor your space to cater to your specific self-care practices and interests, ensuring that everything you need is within arm's reach.

Once your space is transformed, set boundaries around your self-care space to preserve its sacredness. Communicate with those around you that this is your dedicated time and place for self-nurturing. Encourage understanding and respect for your need for privacy and uninterrupted moments of self-care.

Maintain your self-care space with love and attention. Keep it clean, organized, and clutter-free. Regularly update and refresh your symbolic display to reflect your evolving journey. By maintaining your space, you nurture its energy and ensure it remains a sanctuary for your self-love practices.

Creating a space that supports self-care and self-love is a personal and delightful endeavor. Let your creativity flow, infuse your space with elements that resonate with your soul, and make it a reflection of your unique journey. With every intentional touch and loving detail, you are crafting a sanctuary that celebrates and nurtures your self-worth and well-being. Now, go forth and curate your haven of self-care and self-love, my dear seeker of inner harmony.

Setting Up a Social Space

Physical environment isn't enough to fully support the amazing, transformative journey you're experiencing with this book. You also need to nurture relationships with people that will support your endeavors for self-love. Gather 'round as we explore the steps to foster supportive connections.

Start by becoming aware of the people in your life and the impact they have on your well-being. Reflect on how certain relationships make you feel – do they inspire and uplift you, or do they drain your energy? Identifying the dynamics will help you focus on nurturing those connections that contribute positively to your self-love journey.

The next step is to set boundaries. Establishing healthy boundaries is key to maintaining a positive social space. Learn to communicate your needs, desires, and limits to those around you. Respectfully decline activities or engagements that don't align with your self-care goals. Remember, setting boundaries isn't selfish—it's an act of self-love and preservation.

Surround yourself with individuals who genuinely care about your well-being and support your journey of self-love. Look for friends, family members, or even support groups who embrace your growth, offer encouragement, and provide a safe space for vulnerability. Seek out relationships that nourish your soul and make you feel valued.

Openly communicate your intentions and goals for self-love and care with your loved ones. Let them know that you are committed to prioritizing your well-being and seeking their support. By sharing your journey, you allow others to understand and respect your choices, fostering an environment of compassion and encouragement.

Embrace and encourage authenticity within your social circle. Create a space where everyone feels safe to express their true selves without judgment. By celebrating individuality and vulnerability, you create an environment that supports personal growth and self-acceptance.

Actively listen to others when they share their experiences, challenges, and triumphs. Show genuine interest and empathy in their stories. Offer words of encouragement, understanding, or validation. Engaging in active listening cultivates deeper connections and strengthens the support system within your social space.

Embrace a culture of celebration within your social circle. When someone achieves a milestone or experiences personal growth, celebrate their successes wholeheartedly. By joyfully acknowledging each other's accomplishments, you create a positive and uplifting atmosphere that encourages everyone to strive for their own greatness.

Plan activities that align with your self-love and care goals. Engage in mindful practices, such as group meditations or nature walks, that promote well-being and deepen connections. Create opportunities for open dialogue, sharing insights, and learning from one another's experiences. By engaging in meaningful activities together, you nurture a space of growth and mutual support.

Together, you can create an environment where vulnerability, growth, and compassion flourish. Embrace the power of nurturing relationships, for they can become pillars of strength and love as you navigate the beautiful path of self-discovery and care. Now, go forth and curate your social space of love, my dear champion of self-worth and connection!

Conclusion

We've traversed the bountiful lands of self-compassion and self-care, and now we stand at the threshold of Chapter 4, where we shall explore the art of setting boundaries and prioritizing oneself. It's time to don your boundary-setting cape and embark on a journey of self-empowerment and intentional living.

Take a deep breath and remind yourself of your inherent worth and the immense power that lies within you. You have learned to embrace self-compassion, to care for your physical, emotional, mental, and spiritual well-being. Now, it's time to protect and nurture your sacred space by setting boundaries and prioritizing yourself.

Chapter 4 beckons, dear reader, with wisdom and guidance on establishing healthy boundaries that honor your needs, desires, and values. It's time to unveil the secrets of self-preservation and create a life that reflects your authentic self. As we delve into the world of boundaries, prepare to harness the strength to say "no" when it serves your well-being and to say "yes" to the experiences and relationships that nourish your soul.

I implore you to turn the page, for the next chapter awaits. Arm yourself with knowledge, embrace the transformational power of setting boundaries, and embark on a new chapter of self-empowerment. Let us journey together, hand in hand, as you prioritize yourself, carve out your sacred space, and create a life that radiates with authenticity and fulfillment. Onward, my courageous friend!

Takeaways

- Self-compassion is a powerful practice that involves being kind and understanding toward oneself, especially during times of difficulty or failure.
- Practicing self-compassion can lead to improved emotional well-being, increased resilience, and reduced self-criticism.
- Techniques for practicing self-compassion include loving-kindness meditation, self-forgiveness, and mindfulness.
- Physical self-care involves nurturing our bodies through healthy habits, such as exercise, restful sleep, and nourishing nutrition.
- Emotional self-care involves acknowledging and processing our emotions, seeking support when needed, and engaging in activities that bring us joy and fulfillment.
- Mental self-care focuses on nourishing our minds through activities like reading, learning, engaging in creative pursuits, and managing stress.
- Spiritual self-care involves connecting with our inner selves, finding meaning and purpose, and exploring practices that align with our beliefs and values.
- Creating a supportive environment for self-care is essential, whether it's through decluttering our physical space, cultivating positive relationships, or seeking out communities that inspire and uplift us.

CHAPTER 4

SETTING BOUNDARIES AND PRIORITIZING YOURSELF

"Setting boundaries is an act of self-love and self-respect. It's about honoring your needs and creating a space where you can thrive without compromising your well-being." - Unknown

B y establishing and enforcing boundaries, we create a supportive environment that fosters personal growth and maintains healthy relationships. It's a way of expressing self-respect and demonstrating that we deserve to be treated with kindness, understanding, and consideration. Setting boundaries is not selfish; it's an act of self-preservation and an affirmation of our worth.

Setting boundaries and prioritizing yourself are key components of self-love, yet they are often easier said than done. As women, we may feel guilty or selfish for putting our own needs first, leading us to neglect our well-being and compromise our boundaries.

In this chapter, we will explore the importance of setting boundaries to protect your energy and well-being. We'll provide tips for establishing and maintaining healthy boundaries, including the role of assertiveness, self-respect, and consistency. Additionally, we'll cover effective communication strategies for expressing your needs, saying no without guilt, and balancing your work, relationships, and self-care. By learning to prioritize yourself and establish clear boundaries, you can cultivate a sense of inner strength and self-love.

The Importance of Setting Boundaries

If self-love had a superhero cape, setting boundaries would be the golden emblem on its chest. Seriously, these things are powerful! They're like the bouncers at the club of your life, making sure only the right people and experiences get in. So why are boundaries so crucial?

First and foremost, boundaries help protect your precious energy. Think of your energy as a limited resource. You only have so much to go around, and setting boundaries helps you preserve it. When you establish clear boundaries, you create a protective shield around yourself, warding off energy vampires and emotional leeches. No more wasting your energy on toxic relationships or draining situations. It's like a self-care force field!

Secondly, boundaries are essential for preserving your overall well-being. They are the ultimate self-care tool. By setting boundaries, you put your well-being front and center, prioritizing your mental, emotional, and physical health. It's a powerful statement to yourself and others that your well-being matters. Setting boundaries allows you to create a safe space where you can flourish, grow, and nurture yourself.

So, my friend, if you haven't already, it's time to take charge of your life. Protect your energy, preserve your well-being, and create a space where self-love can thrive. Remember, setting boundaries isn't selfish—it's an act of self-care and self-preservation. Embrace your inner bouncer and let the world know that you deserve respect, space, and a life that's in alignment with your needs and values. Get ready to set those boundaries and watch as your self-love soars to new heights!

Tips for Establishing and Maintaining Healthy Boundaries

Let's dive into the wondrous world of setting and nurturing healthy boundaries. Picture yourself as a boundary architect, designing and constructing a fortress of self-care and respect. Here are some essential tips to help you establish and harbor those boundaries like a pro.

Assertiveness

Assertiveness is like having a powerful superhero voice that commands respect and sets clear boundaries. It involves expressing your thoughts, needs, and boundaries in a clear and respectful manner, while also considering the rights and feelings of others. Assertiveness helps you avoid being taken advantage of, feeling overwhelmed, or compromising your well-being for the sake of others. By expressing your boundaries assertively, you set a precedent for how you expect to be treated and you create a healthier dynamic in your relationships. Remember, being assertive doesn't mean being aggressive or confrontational; it's about finding a balance between expressing yourself and respecting others, ultimately fostering healthier and more fulfilling connections. So, how can you unleash your inner assertive badass? Let's dive in:

1. Start with self-awareness: Before you can assert yourself, you need to understand your needs, values, and boundaries. Take some time to reflect on what is important to you and what you are willing to accept or reject in your relationships. This self-awareness will provide a solid foundation for asserting yourself confidently.

2. Practice saying no: Saying "no" is a magical word that can work wonders for setting boundaries. It's like wielding a shield that protects your time, energy, and well-being. Start small by saying no to minor requests or obligations that don't align with your priorities. Remember, saying no doesn't make you mean or selfish—it's an act of self-care and self-respect.

3. Practice active listening: Assertiveness isn't just about speaking up; it's also about listening actively. When engaging in conversations, make an effort to truly hear and understand others. This not only fosters healthy communication but also sets the stage for mutual respect and understanding of each other's boundaries.

4. Set clear consequences: Establishing boundaries without consequences is like having a superhero costume without any superpowers. Be clear about the consequences if your boundaries are not respected. It could be anything from reducing contact with someone who consistently crosses your boundaries to ending a

toxic relationship altogether. Remember, you have the power to protect your boundaries and create a healthier environment for yourself

5. Seek support if needed: If asserting yourself feels challenging or overwhelming, don't hesitate to seek support. Reach out to a trusted friend, family member, or even a therapist who can provide guidance and encouragement. They can offer valuable insights and help you navigate the process of asserting boundaries with confidence.

So, my assertive friend, it's time to unleash your inner superhero voice. Stand tall, communicate your needs and boundaries, and watch as your relationships transform into healthier and more respectful connections. Embrace your assertiveness and create a world where your boundaries are honored, and your self-love thrives.

Self-Respect

Self-respect is a key ingredient in the recipe for healthy boundaries. When you have a strong sense of self-respect, you recognize your inherent value and deservingness of respect, kindness, and consideration in your relationships and interactions. It is the driving force that reminds you to prioritize your needs, set limits, and advocate for yourself in ways that aligns with your values and self-worth. Through practicing self-respect, you cultivate a deep sense of self-love, reinforcing your boundaries and creating a nurturing environment for your personal growth and happiness. This is going to include many techniques that you've already read about so far, so this will mostly be review. Yay you!

1. Value your needs and desires: Treat your needs and desires with the utmost importance. Acknowledge that they matter and deserve to be honored. This means taking the time to identify what truly nourishes and fulfills you, and then communicating those needs to others.

2. Prioritize self-care: Make self-care your number one priority. Set aside dedicated time for activities that recharge and rejuvenate you. Whether it's taking a soothing bath, indulging in a favorite hobby, or simply basking in some alone time, prioritize self-care as an act of self-respect.

3. Surround yourself with supportive people: Surround yourself with individuals who uplift and respect you. Choose relationships where your self-respect is reciprocated. Surrounding yourself with positive influences cultivates an environment where healthy boundaries can thrive.

4. Practice self-acceptance: Embrace yourself fully, flaws and all. Recognize that you are a unique individual with your own strengths and weaknesses. Be kind and compassionate towards yourself and let go of self-judgment or harsh criticism.

5. Speak your truth: Express your thoughts, feelings, and opinions honestly and authentically. Don't shy away from voicing your needs, boundaries, and desires. Speaking your truth not only asserts your self-respect but also fosters open and genuine communication.

6. Practice self-empowerment: Take charge of your life and actively pursue your goals and aspirations. Set achievable targets, break them down into manageable steps, and take action towards

realizing your dreams. Accomplishing what you set out to do boosts your self-respect and self-confidence

7. Practice self-compassion: Treat yourself with kindness, understanding, and forgiveness. Embrace self-compassion when you make mistakes or face challenges. Remember that everyone is imperfect, and self-compassion allows you to learn and grow without diminishing your self-worth.

By incorporating these practices into your life, you'll continue to strengthen your self-respect and cultivate a deep sense of appreciation for yourself. So, go forth and rock your self-respect like the superhero you are!

Consistency

The final ingredient: consistency. When you consistently enforce your boundaries, it eliminates any confusion or mixed signals that may arise from inconsistent boundary-setting. By being consistent, you provide a reliable framework for everyone to understand and respect your boundaries. When you consistently uphold your boundaries, it demonstrates that you mean what you say. People learn to trust that you will follow through and stick to your boundaries. This fosters trust and credibility in your relationships, as others see you as someone who is reliable and true to their word. In a nutshell, consistency in setting and upholding boundaries is like the secret ingredient that makes them effective. It establishes clarity, builds trust, and reinforces your self-worth. So, put on your consistency cape and let it guide you in creating a boundary superhero version of yourself!

1. Be clear and consistent in your communication: Clearly express your boundaries and expectations to others and be consistent in how you communicate them. This means avoiding mixed messages and being firm in your stance.

2. Follow through with consequences: When someone crosses your boundaries, it's important to enforce the consequences you've established. Whether it's setting limits on your availability or addressing disrespectful behavior, consistency in enforcing consequences reinforces the importance of your boundaries.

3. Seek support and accountability: Surround yourself with individuals who respect and understand the importance of boundaries. Share your journey with them and ask for their support and accountability in maintaining consistent boundaries.

Remember, consistency takes time and effort. It's about establishing a pattern of behavior that aligns with your values and needs. By consistently upholding your boundaries, you send a powerful message to others about your self-worth and create an environment that respects and supports your well-being.

Communicating Your Needs Effectively

So, you know what you need to do, but many people struggle with the very first step in setting boundaries: communicating what the boundaries are. Often, women will struggle with communicating their wants and needs in a way that is clear and effective, for fear of sounding unrelenting and uncompromising.

I'm here to tell you that you just gotta do it. Doing these things is never easy, but trust me, you're going to be glad that you did.

When it comes to effectively communicating your needs, it's all about being direct and clear. No need to beat around the bush or rely on secret codes. Just say what you mean and mean what you say. Remember, people can't read your mind (unless you've discovered a new superpower, in which case, please share!).

Use "I" statements to express how you feel and what you need. Instead of pointing fingers and playing the blame game, focus on expressing your own emotions and desires. This way, you take ownership of your needs without putting others on the defensive. It's like being the captain of your own ship, steering it in the direction that serves you best. So, ditch the vague hints and speak up with confidence!

Be confident, but not a dictator. Assertiveness is key when communicating your needs, but that doesn't mean you need to turn into a demanding diva. Find a balance between being firm and respectful. Speak your truth with confidence, but also be open to listening and understanding the perspectives of others. It's like doing a graceful dance where you express yourself while still being considerate of those around you.

You also need to think fully about what you're going to say before you say it. Use your words wisely. Remember, effective communication is not about launching verbal grenades at others. It's about expressing your needs and desires in a way that fosters understanding and connection. Choose your words carefully, aiming for clarity and kindness. Keep in mind that your goal is to create healthy boundaries, not to start a verbal war.

When it comes to communicating your own needs, active listening allows you to gain a deeper understanding of yourself and your desires. By actively listening to your inner voice and paying attention to your own thoughts and emotions, you become more aware of what you truly need and want in different situations.

Additionally, active listening helps you respond more effectively when expressing your needs to others. By understanding their perspective and needs through active listening, you can tailor your communication to resonate with them. This creates a cooperative and respectful environment where both parties feel acknowledged and understood.

By practicing these communication techniques, you'll become a boundary-setting maestro, adept at expressing your needs with confidence and clarity. So, go forth and communicate like a boss (a friendly and considerate boss, of course)!

Saying No Without Guilt

Yes, the age-old struggle of saying "no" without feeling guilty, especially for women. Well, here's the deal: saying "no" is not a crime, and it certainly doesn't make you a bad person. In fact, it's an essential skill for setting boundaries and taking care of yourself.

To say "no" assertively and without guilt, start by recognizing that your needs and well-being are just as important as anyone else's. Remind yourself that you have the right to prioritize yourself and your own happiness. It's not selfish; it's self-care.

Next, practice saying "no" with confidence and clarity. Be direct, yet polite, in your response. You don't have to justify or apologize excessively for your decision. Remember, you're not obligated to give a lengthy explanation for your boundaries.

It can also be helpful to set realistic expectations for yourself. Accept that you can't please everyone all the time, and that's perfectly okay. Embrace the fact that you're not responsible for fulfilling every request or meeting every demand. Focus on what aligns with your values and priorities.

Another tip is to, yet again, practice self-compassion! Bet you didn't see that coming. It's natural to feel a twinge of guilt when you first start saying "no" more assertively. But remember, it's not about rejecting others; it's about honoring yourself. Remind yourself that your needs matter and that taking care of yourself is a worthy pursuit.

So, take a deep breath, embrace your assertiveness, and let go of that unnecessary guilt. Say "no" when you need to, with confidence and self-assurance. It's your life, and you have every right to shape it according to your own needs and desires.

Overcoming the Fear of Rejection and Disappointment

Fear and disappointment are a common concern when it comes to setting and enforcing healthy boundaries, especially when it may lead to the termination of friendships or relationships. But fear not, my friend! Let's tackle this in a supportive and empowering way.

First, remind yourself that your well-being and happiness should be a priority. It's okay to put yourself first and establish boundaries that serve your needs. Embrace the idea that you deserve to be surrounded by people who respect and support you.

Secondly, understand that not everyone will respond positively to your boundaries, and that's okay. The truth is that healthy boundaries can be a litmus test for the quality of your relationships. Those who truly care about you and value your friendship will respect and understand your boundaries, even if it requires some adjustment on their part.

However, if someone reacts negatively or rejects your boundaries, it's important to recognize that it may not be a reflection of your worth or value. It may simply indicate that the relationship was not built on mutual respect and understanding. In such cases, it's okay to mourn the loss and acknowledge your feelings of disappointment, but also remember that it creates space for healthier and more fulfilling connections to enter your life.

To overcome the fear of rejection and disappointment, cultivate self-compassion and self-esteem (hey, you know those ones!) Remind yourself of your own worth and surround yourself with supportive and uplifting individuals who appreciate and honor your boundaries. Focus on building relationships that are based on mutual respect, trust, and understanding.

Lastly, remember that boundaries are not meant to keep people out, but rather to create a healthier and more balanced dynamic. Embrace the belief that by setting and enforcing healthy boundaries, you're creating space for more authentic and fulfilling connections in your life. Trust yourself, stay true to your needs, and remember that you deserve relationships that uplift and empower you.

Balancing Work, Relationships and Self-Care

The eternal juggling act of work, relationships, and self-care is hard; trust me, I know. It's like trying to balance a flaming sword on one hand while juggling pineapples with the other. Quite the challenge, my friend! Add in a second sword if you're a mother; it seems impossible! But fear not, for I shall guide you through this delicate dance with a touch of humor and wisdom.

First, let's acknowledge the importance of balance. Research suggests that maintaining a healthy work-life balance is essential for overall well-being and happiness (Smith & Hughes, 2019). So, let's dive into some practical tips on how to balance these three elements like a graceful acrobat.

1. Prioritize and delegate: Start by identifying your top priorities in each area—work, relationships, and self-care. Determine what truly matters to you and focus your energy accordingly. Learn to delegate tasks and ask for help when it's needed. Remember, you don't have to be a superhero who does it all. These tasks may all seem important, but I promise, they aren't.

2. Schedule self-care: Treat self-care like a hot date with yourself. Schedule dedicated time for activities that nourish your mind, body, and soul. Whether it's reading a book, taking a bubble bath, or practicing yoga, make self-care a non-negotiable priority. After all, you can't pour from an empty cup.

3. Communicate openly: Effective communication is key to maintaining balance. Be open and honest with your boss, colleagues, and loved ones about your needs and limitations. Let them know when you need support or flexibility. Remember, you're not a mind reader, and neither are they!

4. Practice mindfulness: Embrace the power of mindfulness to stay present and focused. Take moments throughout the day to check in with yourself, breathe deeply, and release any tension. Mindfulness can help you navigate the chaos with grace and keep your sanity intact.

5. Seek support: Don't be afraid to lean on your support network. Reach out to friends, family, or even seek professional help when needed. Surround yourself with people who lift you up and provide guidance. Remember, you don't have to do it alone, and a little help goes a long way.

Balance is like walking a tightrope, but with practice, patience, and a sprinkle of self-compassion, you can find your equilibrium. Embrace the challenges, embrace the laughter, and remember that you are the ringmaster of your own circus. Now go forth, juggle those pineapples, and conquer the world with your magnificent balancing act!

Conclusion

Congratulations on reaching the end of Chapter 4, my fellow self-love enthusiast! But wait, there's more to explore on this wonderful journey of self-discovery. In Chapter 5, we delve into the realm of strengthening relationships through self-love. So, grab your metaphorical cape and let's dive right in!

We'll explore how embracing self-love can lead to healthier connections, improved communication, and a deeper understanding of yourself and others. Get ready to unlock the secrets of building stronger bonds while nourishing your own soul. Discover how self-love can create a ripple effect, transforming not only your relationship with yourself but also your relationships with your loved ones.

So, my friend, take a deep breath, pat yourself on the back for the progress you've made so far, and get ready for Chapter 5. Strengthen your relationships, ignite the power of self-love, and let's embark on this beautiful journey together. Trust me, the best is yet to come!

Takeaways

- Setting boundaries is crucial for protecting your energy and well-being.
- Assertiveness plays a vital role in establishing healthy boundaries and communicating your needs effectively.
- Self-respect is essential in maintaining and enforcing boundaries, showing others how you deserve to be treated.
- Consistency is key when it comes to upholding your boundaries and ensuring they are respected.
- Active listening is a powerful tool for effective communication, allowing you to understand others and be understood.
- Learning to say no without guilt is empowering and necessary for preserving your time and energy.
- Overcoming the fear of rejection and disappointment involves embracing your worth and understanding that healthy boundaries are necessary for your well-being.
- Balancing work, relationships, and self-care requires prioritization, time management, and self-compassion.

CHAPTER 5

STRENGTHENING RELATIONSHIPS THROUGH SELF-LOVE

"Love is not about finding the right person, but about being the right person. When we embrace self-love and nurture our own well-being, we bring our best selves to our relationships, creating a foundation of love, trust, and growth." - Unknown

Healthy relationships are a vital component of a fulfilling life, yet they can be a source of stress and negativity if not approached with intention and self-love.

In this chapter, we will explore how self-love can strengthen our relationships, from attracting positive connections to recognizing and breaking patterns of toxic relationships. We'll provide tips for fostering mutual support and growth in relationships through open communication, trust, and empathy, and explore the importance of vulnerability in building intimacy with others. Additionally, we'll cover practical strategies for maintaining harmony in relationships, including practicing forgiveness, compromise, and acceptance. By approaching our relationships with a foundation of self-love, we can create a network of positive connections that support and empower us.

Attracting Healthy Relationships

In the journey of strengthening relationships through self-love, it's important to focus on identifying and cultivating positive connections. By surrounding ourselves with supportive, loving, and uplifting individuals, we create an environment that nurtures our self-worth and growth. Here are some key aspects to consider:

Assessing existing relationships is the first step. Take a close look at the relationships in your life and evaluate their impact on your well-being. Identify those that bring positivity, respect, and support, and those that may be toxic or draining. This awareness helps you make informed decisions about the relationships you want to nurture. You can even use the things that you've learned so far and apply it to past relationships. In what area were the two of you lacking?

Setting boundaries is crucial for healthy relationships. Luckily for you, you just learned how to do that! This is an extremely important tool that you need to use in your newfound self-love based relationships. Establish clear boundaries that protect your emotional and mental well-being. Communicate your needs and expectations and be assertive in enforcing those boundaries. It's essential to prioritize your own needs and to not compromise on your values or well-being. This is going to be an area of your life where setting boundaries is most important!

Cultivating positive connections involves actively seeking out individuals who align with your values, interests, and aspirations. Engage in activities and communities where you can meet like-minded people and build meaningful connections. Surrounding yourself with individuals who inspire and support you is instrumental in strengthening your relationships.

Embracing authenticity is key. Be true to yourself and allow others to see your genuine self. Authenticity fosters deeper connections and attracts relationships with people who appreciate and value you for who you truly are. When you embrace your authentic self, you attract people who celebrate your uniqueness.

Nurturing healthy dynamics is essential in any relationship. Focus on fostering relationships built on mutual respect, trust, and support. Encourage open and honest communication, active listening, and empathy in your interactions. By creating a safe and nurturing space for both yourself and others, you cultivate relationships that flourish and grow.

Now, I know that's easier said than done. Sometimes it's hard for people to recognize what healthy dynamics are, or how to properly communicate them in a relationship. Practically nurturing healthy dynamics in your relationships is all about applying what you've learned so far in this book. Here are some practical tips to put into action:

1. Practice effective communication: Use your newfound assertiveness and active listening skills to communicate openly

and honestly with your loved ones. Express your thoughts, feelings, and needs clearly and respectfully, while also being receptive to their perspectives.

2. Set and maintain boundaries: Continue to establish and enforce healthy boundaries in your relationships. Be clear about your limits and communicate them assertively. Remember, boundaries are not meant to push people away but to create a space where both parties feel respected and understood.

3. Celebrate imperfections: Embrace your own imperfections and extend that acceptance to others. Recognize that nobody is perfect, including yourself and those around you. Choose understanding over judgment and provide support in moments of vulnerability.

4. Show appreciation and gratitude: Take time to express your appreciation and gratitude for the people in your life. Let them know how much you value their presence and the positive impact they have on you. Small gestures of kindness and gratitude go a long way in nurturing healthy dynamics.

5. Practice self-care: Remember to prioritize self-care and self-love as you navigate your relationships. Take time for yourself, engage in activities that bring you joy, and ensure you're meeting your own needs. When you're in a good place mentally, emotionally, and physically, you can contribute more positively to your relationships.

6. Seek support when needed: Don't hesitate to reach out for support when you're facing challenges or need guidance. Whether it's through trusted friends, family, or professional help, having a support system can provide valuable insights and assistance in nurturing healthy dynamics.

Remember, building and nurturing healthy dynamics is an ongoing process that requires effort and commitment. Embrace the lessons you've learned, maintain a playful and friendly approach, and continue to cultivate relationships that bring out the best in you and your loved ones.

Attracting healthy relationships is not about changing who you are, but rather aligning yourself with people who appreciate and celebrate your uniqueness. Prioritizing self-love and building a strong foundation within yourself allows you to cultivate strong, uplifting connections with others.

Recognizing and Breaking Patterns of Toxic Relationships

Transitioning into a section on recognizing and breaking patterns of toxic relationships, it's important to understand the impact such relationships can have on our well-being. Toxic relationships are characterized by patterns of negativity, manipulation, and emotional harm that can drain our energy and hinder our personal growth. By recognizing these patterns and taking action, we can free ourselves from toxic dynamics and pave the way for healthier connections.

Awareness

Becoming aware of the patterns of a toxic relationship is an important step towards breaking free from its harmful effects. One way to develop this awareness is by reflecting on your feelings. Pay attention to how you feel when you're with the person in question. Do you often feel drained, anxious, or unhappy? Trust your instincts and acknowledge any negative emotions that arise.

Another approach is to notice recurring patterns. Look for consistent behaviors that cause distress or harm in the relationship. This could include patterns of manipulation, disrespect, or control. By recognizing these patterns, you can begin to see the toxic dynamics at play. It's crucial to pay attention to red flags and warning signs. These may include consistent disrespect, manipulation, excessive criticism, emotional or physical abuse, constant negativity, and a lack of trust or support. Trust your intuition and acknowledge your feelings if something doesn't feel right or if you find yourself constantly unhappy or drained in a particular relationship.

Additionally, seeking feedback from trusted friends or family members can provide valuable insights. They may have observed unhealthy patterns that you might have missed. Be open to their perspectives and consider their observations in evaluating the dynamics of your relationship.

Journaling can also be a helpful tool. Take time to write about your experiences, feelings, and observations. This can provide clarity and help you identify patterns over time.

Remember, developing awareness takes time and self-reflection. The goal is to gain a clearer understanding of the toxic patterns in your relationship so that you can take steps towards breaking free and cultivating healthier connections.

Healing

Breaking patterns of toxic relationships starts with setting firm boundaries and prioritizing your well-being. This may involve limiting or cutting off contact with toxic individuals, seeking support from trusted friends or professionals, and engaging in self-reflection to understand your own role in perpetuating these patterns. Recognize that ending toxic relationships is an act of self-love and self-respect, even if it may be difficult or uncomfortable in the short term.

As you distance yourself from toxic dynamics, focus on healing and rebuilding. First and foremost, give yourself permission to feel. It's completely normal to experience a range of emotions after leaving a toxic relationship. You might feel relieved, sad, angry, or even confused. Allow yourself to process these emotions without judgment. Give yourself the time and space to heal.

During this healing process, it's essential to prioritize self-care. Take care of your physical, emotional, and mental well-being. Engage in activities that bring you joy and relaxation. Surround yourself with positive and supportive people who lift you up.

Consider seeking professional support as well. Therapy or counseling can provide a safe and supportive space to explore your experiences, heal from any trauma, and gain valuable insights into yourself and your relationship patterns. Healing takes time, and there will be ups and downs along the way. Celebrate your progress, no matter how small it may seem. Allow yourself to grow and evolve as an individual.

Lastly, keep focusing on self-love and self-compassion. Remind yourself that you are worthy of love and happiness. Surround yourself with positive affirmations, practice self-care, and celebrate your strengths and accomplishments.

Remember, you're not alone in this journey. Reach out to friends, family, or support groups who can offer understanding and encouragement. You deserve healthy and fulfilling relationships, and with time and self-care, you will heal and create a brighter future for yourself.

Self-Protection

All of these values and tips will allow you to self-protect against future toxic relationship patterns. How can you prioritize it?

First and foremost, establish and enforce clear boundaries, duh! Identify what is acceptable and unacceptable behavior for you in any relationship as soon as possible. These are things that any potential partner should know early on. Communicate your boundaries assertively and confidently and be prepared to enforce them if they are crossed. Remember, your boundaries are there to protect your emotional and mental well-being. It's also important to set boundaries moving forward. You deserve to be treated with respect, kindness, and love.

Learn to trust your instincts. After being in a toxic relationship, you might have doubts or fears about entering new relationships, and that's completely normal! On the other end, make sure to listen to everything that you've learned and pay attention to any red flags that arise. Trusting yourself and your intuition will help you navigate relationships with more confidence and protect yourself from potential harm.

Continuous reflection is key. Use every period of singleness as an opportunity to understand the patterns and dynamics that contributed to the toxicity that you've experienced in the past. Reflect on any warning signs you may have ignored or compromised on. This self-reflection will help you make wiser choices and protect yourself from similar situations in the future.

Practice self-care as an act of self-protection, and you already know how! Nurture your physical, emotional, and mental well-being. Engage in activities that bring you joy, prioritize rest and relaxation, and invest in practices that promote self-love and self-compassion. Taking care of yourself helps to build resilience and safeguards your overall well-being.

Remember, self-protection also means saying no when necessary. Be comfortable asserting your boundaries and saying no to situations or relationships that don't align with your values or contribute to your growth and happiness. Trust that you have the right to prioritize yourself and your well-being.

Finally, celebrate your journey and the strength it took to break free. Recognize your progress and accomplishments. You've taken a significant step toward a healthier and happier life. Be kind to yourself, be patient, and know that you deserve to be protected, respected, and cherished.

Always remember that you have the power to protect yourself and create a better future. I'm here for you every step of the way, cheering you on and supporting you. You deserve all the love, happiness, and security in the world. Keep shining, my friend!

Fostering Mutual Support and Growth in Relationships

Building healthy and fulfilling connections with others is such a crucial part of our journey towards self-love and personal growth. When it comes to fostering mutual support and growth in relationships, it's all about creating an environment where both you and your loved ones can thrive and flourish. It's about nurturing connections that inspire growth, provide a safe space for vulnerability, and encourage each other to become the best versions of ourselves.

So often, relationships can become stagnant or even toxic if there's a lack of support and growth. That's why we want to focus on cultivating an environment that nourishes personal development and allows for open and honest communication.

So, get ready to embark on this journey of fostering mutual support and growth in your relationships. Let's learn, grow, and create the kind of connections that uplift and empower us. You deserve to be surrounded by people who truly support and celebrate you, and I'm excited to help you make that a reality.

Open Communication

Open communication is a key ingredient in fostering mutual support and growth in relationships. It's all about creating a safe space where you and your loved ones can express yourselves honestly, share your needs and desires, and actively listen to one another. So, let's talk about how you can cultivate open communication in your relationships.

To encourage open communication, you need to start with self-awareness. Before you can communicate effectively with others, it's important to understand your own feelings, needs, and boundaries. Take the time to reflect on what you truly want to express and what's important to you; if you need to go back and read the chapter with self-awareness again, that's totally fine. Don't worry, I'll be right here waiting for you.

Next, you need to work on the environment of your relationship, creating a safe and judgment-free zone. Establish an environment where both parties feel safe and respected. Encourage open dialogue by being non-judgmental, avoiding criticism, and focusing on understanding rather than assigning blame.

Once your environment is good to go, it's time to pull out your skills with active listening. Communication doesn't work unless both parties are both speaking and listening, *really* listening. When your loved ones are speaking, give them your full attention. Show genuine interest, maintain eye contact, and avoid interrupting. Reflect back what you've understood to ensure clarity and demonstrate that you value their perspective.

Next, here's assertiveness again! I know it's terrifying, but the more you practice, the better at it you'll be. Express yourself in a direct yet respectful manner. Use "I" statements to express your feelings and needs without blaming or attacking the other person. For example, say, "I feel hurt when..." rather than "You always make me feel..."

If you've gotten this far, congrats! You've been able to communicate effectively on your end. On the other end, you need to make sure that they feel safe to respond to you. Welcome and encourage open communication. Let them know that you're open to hearing their thoughts, feelings, and concerns without judgment. Be patient and give them the space to express themselves fully.

Okay, so they might have said something that offended you. Oops! I know it may seem like a toxic trait if your partner offends you, but it's usually not intentional. Seek to understand the perspective of your loved ones. Put yourself in their shoes, validate their feelings, and show empathy. This creates a supportive atmosphere where both parties feel heard and understood.

Okay, so you did all the communicating you can, but a conflict still occurred. What now? Conflict is a natural part of any relationship. When disagreements arise, approach them with a problem-solving mindset. Focus on finding common ground, compromising, and seeking win-win solutions. Avoid personal attacks and strive for a resolution that benefits both parties.

Remember, open communication is a two-way street. Encourage your loved ones to also practice these principles, creating a dynamic of mutual understanding and support. By fostering open communication, you can build stronger connections, enhance trust, and create an environment where both you and your loved ones can grow and thrive together. But this will only happen if it occurs on both sides. You should view it as a red flag when your partner is completely unwilling to try any of these techniques, refusing to change their thought and behavior patterns.

Trust

Trust is the foundation of strong and healthy relationships. Building and fostering trust is essential for mutual support and growth. It's especially hard to rebuild trust after it's already been broken, and if you're there, I feel you. These steps may be harder for you and your loved ones to adjust to, but the rewards are worth it. There's no point in having a relationship with anyone if you don't trust them.

The first part of trust is to show up for your loved ones consistently and be reliable. Be someone they can count on in both good times and bad. Keep your promises and commitments and be there when they need you. This builds a sense of reliability and strengthens trust.

Not only does trust have to exist in your actions, but it has to be apparent in your words. Be honest and transparent in your communication. Avoid hiding or withholding important information. Share your thoughts, feelings, and intentions openly, even if it feels vulnerable. Honesty promotes trust and authenticity in your relationships, even if you're afraid to be open or hurt someone's feelings. Honesty always works better in the long run, even if it doesn't seem like it at the moment.

Engaging in behaviors that actively build trust is essential, especially for those who are trying to rebuild it after it's been broken. For example, respecting boundaries, maintaining confidentiality, and being loyal are some basic blocks toward building trust. Demonstrate your trustworthiness through your actions and choices consistently.

Trust can only continue if everyone involved realizes that we're never going to be perfect. Mistakes happen in relationships. When trust is broken, be willing to forgive and work towards repair. Address conflicts and breaches of trust directly and openly, seeking resolution and understanding. Practice empathy and compassion during the process.

Now, you can't trust someone else if you don't trust yourself. Trusting yourself is just as important as trusting others. Be self-aware, honor your boundaries, and make choices that are aligned with your values. When you trust yourself, others are more likely to trust you as well.

Remember, trust takes time to build and can be easily damaged. Be patient, understanding, and committed to nurturing trust in your relationships. Trust is the glue that strengthens mutual support and growth, creating a foundation of security and connection.

Empathy

Empathy is a powerful tool for fostering mutual support and growth in relationships. It allows us to understand and connect with others on a deeper level, and the first step is always to develop an ability to look at things from someone else's perspective.

Hello, active listening again! I know you've heard it multiple times by now, but it's important! Give your full attention, maintain eye contact, and be present in the conversation. Avoid interrupting or formulating responses in your mind while the other person is speaking. Try to see the situation from the other person's perspective. Imagine how they might be feeling and what they might be going through. This helps you develop a greater understanding and empathy for their experiences.

Besides active listening, you have to actually listen and respond to what your loved one is feeling. Show empathy by validating the other person's feelings, letting them know that their emotions are valid and that you understand. Avoid dismissing or minimizing their experiences, just as if you wouldn't want someone to minimize yours.

Just because you're trying to show empathy, doesn't mean you aren't allowed to question someone's thoughts or feelings. If you're unsure about something or want to better understand the other person's point of view, ask questions. This demonstrates your genuine interest and willingness to learn more about their thoughts and feelings and will actually make your partner feel more heard and seen by you.

Now, if you want to double boost your empathetic skills, use both verbal and non-verbal cues to express empathy. Verbalize your understanding and support, and use non-verbal gestures such as nodding, smiling, or gentle touches to convey your empathy.

None of this will work if you don't know what you might bring to the situation. Developing self-awareness and reflecting on your own biases, assumptions, and reactions is a crucial step in practicing empathy. Being aware of your own emotional triggers can help you respond with empathy rather than defensiveness or judgment.

Remember, empathy is a skill that can be developed and strengthened over time. By practicing empathy, you create a supportive and nurturing environment in your relationships, fostering mutual growth, understanding, and connection.

Building Intimacy Through Vulnerability

Now, all the work you've done so far are perfect ways to build intimacy in your relationship. Trust, empathy and open communication are key ways to build both vulnerability and intimacy, contributing to your connection with others. It involves opening up, sharing your authentic self, and allowing others to do the same. The only thing that's missing is developing and celebrating your authentic self and encouraging it from your relationships.

You might be asking, "how do I develop my authenticity? What does that even mean?" Well, let me explain it to you.

Authenticity starts by accepting and embracing your own vulnerabilities. Recognizing that it's natural to have fears, insecurities, and imperfections pushes you towards embracing every part of yourself and letting go of the need for perfection. From there, you ensure that you are communicating all those parts of yourself to your partner. But why? Why does your partner need this from you to feel close to you?

When you are authentic, you allow your partner to see and know the real you. You are honest and transparent about your thoughts, feelings, and experiences, creating an environment where your partner feels comfortable doing the same. This deepens the emotional connection and allows for a richer and more meaningful bond.

Authenticity also promotes acceptance and understanding between partners. Allowing your partner to see your strengths, weaknesses, and quirks helps them understand and accept you for who you truly are, fostering a sense of unconditional love.

On a statistical front, authenticity contributes to long-term relationship satisfaction. When both partners can be authentic and true to themselves, it leads to a sense of fulfillment and happiness in the relationship. Authenticity helps you create a relationship where you can grow and evolve together.

In summary, authenticity is important for developing intimacy in a relationship because it cultivates genuine connection, trust, emotional depth, and acceptance. By being true to yourself and allowing your partner to do the same, you create a strong and fulfilling bond built on love, understanding, and authenticity. So where can you start?

Begin with sharing smaller, less intimidating vulnerabilities and gradually work your way towards deeper disclosures. This gradual process allows trust to be built and nurtures a sense of emotional safety. After you have a handle on it, you can offer genuine emotional support to your partner when they express their vulnerabilities, showing understanding and reassuring them that you are there for them.

While vulnerability is important, it's crucial to respect each other's boundaries. Allow your partner to disclose at their own pace and comfort level. Avoid pressuring or forcing vulnerability and acknowledge moments of vulnerability in your relationship. Celebrate the courage it takes to be vulnerable and reinforce the safe space you've created.

Maintaining Relationship Harmony

Alright, time to talk about maintaining relationship harmony! We all know that even the best relationships can hit a few bumps along the way. But fear not, because this section is all about keeping that love train on track and ensuring smooth sailing. So, buckle up and get ready for some tips and tricks to maintain that sweet, sweet harmony in your relationships.

Practicing Forgiveness

Forgiveness, the secret sauce for relationship harmony. We've all had those moments when our partners do something that irks us. Maybe they forget to take out the trash (again) or accidentally spill coffee on our favorite shirt. But hey, life happens, right? Practicing forgiveness is like hitting the reset button on our emotional scoreboard. It's about letting go of grudges, releasing the need to be right all the time, and opening our hearts to understanding and compassion. So, next time your partner messes up, take a deep breath, channel your inner Zen master, and let forgiveness work its magic. Remember, no relationship is perfect, but forgiveness sure does keep the love train chugging along! Choo-choo!

Compromise

Compromise is like a dance where both partners take turns leading and following. Sometimes you want sushi for dinner, but your partner is craving pizza. What's a couple to do? Well, compromise is the answer! It's about finding creative solutions that satisfy both parties. Maybe you order sushi this time and promise to have pizza night next week. Or perhaps you try a fusion restaurant that offers both sushi and pizza. The key is to be flexible, open-minded, and willing to meet halfway. Remember, relationships are a two-way street, and compromise keeps the traffic flowing smoothly.

I totally get where you're coming from when you feel like you're the one doing all the compromising in your relationship. It can be frustrating and leave you wondering if it's fair or sustainable in the long run.

First off, it's important to acknowledge your feelings and concerns. It's perfectly valid to want a balanced give-and-take in a relationship. Open and honest communication is key here. Sit down with your partner and express how you've been feeling, emphasizing the importance of finding a middle ground where both of you can meet each other's needs.

Next, it's time to explore the dynamics of compromise in your relationship. Reflect on whether there might be any patterns or habits that contribute to you feeling like you're always the one compromising. Are there certain areas where you're more willing to compromise, while your partner tends to hold firm? Understanding these dynamics can help you address them and work towards a more balanced approach.

Encourage your partner to take an active role in finding solutions and compromising as well. Remember, healthy relationships are built on mutual respect and understanding. It's crucial to create an environment where both partners can freely express their needs and concerns, and work together to find compromises that feel fair and satisfying.

Finding a balance in compromise can be an ongoing process, but with open communication, mutual understanding, and a willingness from both sides, it's possible to create a more equitable dynamic. So, my friend, keep those lines of communication open, be assertive about your needs, and don't be afraid to advocate for yourself. You deserve a relationship that's built on reciprocity and respect.

Acceptance

Acceptance involves embracing the quirks and idiosyncrasies of your partner with open arms. Picture this: your partner has a knack for leaving their socks scattered around the house, no matter how many times you've politely asked them not to. Instead of getting frustrated and launching a sock-hunting mission, try a sprinkle of acceptance. Recognize that we're all imperfect beings with our own little habits. Embrace the fact that your partner's quirks are what make them unique and lovable. Take a deep breath, let go of the need for control, and choose acceptance. After all, socks can be picked up, but a strong and harmonious relationship is a treasure worth cherishing.

Oh, believe me, I hear you loud and clear when you say "easier said than done" about acceptance. It's true, accepting someone fully and unconditionally can be challenging, especially when their actions or behaviors test your patience. But hey, let's be real here: relationships are all about growth and compromise. Embracing acceptance is a journey, and it takes time and effort from both partners.

Start by reminding yourself that acceptance doesn't mean you have to tolerate harmful behavior or compromise your own values. It's about acknowledging and embracing the differences that make your partner who they are. It's about understanding that they have their own set of strengths and weaknesses, just like you do.

Take baby steps towards acceptance. Practice empathy and try to see things from your partner's perspective. Communicate openly and honestly about your feelings and needs and encourage them to do the same. Embrace the art of compromise, finding middle ground where both of you can feel respected and heard.

Remember, acceptance is a continuous process, and it won't happen overnight. But as you work on it together, you'll find that it strengthens the foundation of your relationship and allows for deeper understanding and for love to flourish. So, my friend, take a deep breath, be patient with yourself and your partner, and let acceptance unfold one step at a time. You've got this!

Conclusion

Congratulations on reaching the final chapter of this journey towards self-love and personal growth! In Chapter 6, we delve into the power of embracing vulnerability and building resilience. It's time to explore the strength that lies within you as you open yourself up to new possibilities and navigate life's challenges with grace and resilience. Are you ready to dive in and discover your true potential? Let's embark on this final chapter together and unlock the incredible power of vulnerability and resilience in your life. Get ready to embrace your inner strength and soar to new heights of self-love and fulfillment.

Takeaways

- Cultivating positive connections is key to attracting healthy relationships.
- Recognize and break patterns of toxic relationships for your well-being.
- Healing after a toxic relationship involves self-care, self-reflection, and seeking support.
- Self-protection is crucial to maintain boundaries and prioritize your well-being.
- Foster mutual support and growth through open communication, trust, empathy, and authenticity.
- Build intimacy in your relationships by embracing vulnerability.
- Maintain relationship harmony through forgiveness, compromise, and acceptance

CHAPTER 6

EMBRACING VULNERABILITY AND BUILDING RESILIENCE

"Vulnerability is not winning or losing; it's having the courage to show up and be seen when we have no control over the outcome." - Brené Brown

By embracing vulnerability and building resilience, we open ourselves up to deeper connections, personal growth, and the ability to navigate challenges with strength and grace.

Vulnerability and resilience are two sides of the same coin, both essential for building a life rooted in self-love.

In this chapter, we will explore the power of vulnerability, the courage to be imperfect and authentic, and how it can help us overcome setbacks and challenges. You'll get tips for developing coping strategies and support networks, as well as cultivating confidence through self-love, overcoming self-doubt, and embracing your potential. We'll also cover the importance of building resilience, learning from failures, and adapting to change. Finally, we'll discuss how leaving a legacy of self-love can empower future generations of women to embrace their own vulnerability and build resilience in the face of life's challenges.

The Power of Vulnerability

We've explored how vulnerability allows us to embrace our imperfections and show up authentically in our relationships and lives. It takes courage to be vulnerable, to let go of the fear of judgment and rejection, and instead, lean into our true selves. By embracing vulnerability, we create opportunities for deeper connections, increased self-awareness, and personal growth.

Remember the lessons we've discussed earlier in the book. Embrace self-compassion, practice setting healthy boundaries, and nurture supportive relationships. Understand that vulnerability is not a weakness but a strength that allows us to cultivate resilience and experience genuine connection. So, let's harness the power of vulnerability, as well as the courage to be imperfect and authentic, as we continue on our journey towards self-love and personal fulfillment. You've already come so far, and I believe in your ability to embrace vulnerability and build resilience like a champion!

Overcoming Setbacks and Challenges

Life is full of ups and downs, but with the right tools and a strong support system, we can navigate through difficult times more effectively. So, let's explore some practical strategies and the role of support networks in building resilience.

Developing healthy coping mechanisms for challenges and setbacks is an essential part of building resilience and maintaining well-being. Here are some practical ways the reader can cultivate healthy coping strategies, most of which you've already read about so far, but review is always good!

Coping Mechanisms

1. Practice self-care: Sound familiar? Engage in activities that bring you joy, relaxation, and rejuvenation like hobbies, exercise, spending time in nature, practicing mindfulness or meditation, or enjoying a soothing bath. As you probably know by now, taking care of your physical, emotional, and mental well-being is crucial during challenging times. Even if you don't want to, refer to that list of go-to self-care techniques and reset!

2. Seek support: Reach out to trusted friends, family members, or a support network when you're facing difficulties. Sharing your thoughts and feelings with others can provide comfort, validation, and different perspectives. Don't hesitate to seek professional help if needed, such as counseling or therapy, to gain additional support and guidance.

3. Practice emotional awareness: Self-awareness is here to stay! When you're dealing with tough times, it's important to acknowledge that it's normal to feel a range of emotions during challenging situations. Journaling, talking with a trusted confidant, or engaging in expressive activities like art or music can help you explore and express your emotions in a healthy way.

4. Remember your growth mindset: Look for opportunities for growth and learning in setbacks, and practice gratitude by

focusing on the positive aspects of your life, even in difficult times. Write down how you can learn and grow from this experience.

5. Set realistic expectations: Be mindful of setting realistic expectations for yourself and others, recognizing that everyone faces challenges and setbacks, and it's okay to take things one step at a time. You got this!

Support Systems

In addition to coping mechanisms, developing a support network is crucial for embracing challenges and building resilience. Here are some steps the reader can take to create and nurture a supportive network:

1. Identify trusted individuals: Start by identifying the people in your life whom you trust and feel comfortable opening up to. This could include friends, family members, colleagues, mentors, or support groups. Consider the individuals who have shown empathy, understanding, and support in the past.

2. Foster reciprocity: Building a strong support network involves reciprocity. Be willing to offer support and be there for others when they need it. Cultivate meaningful connections by being a reliable and compassionate presence in their lives as well.

3. Join supportive communities: Seek out support groups or communities that align with your interests, values, or specific challenges you're facing. These communities can provide a sense of belonging, understanding, and shared experiences. Whether it's an online group, a local meetup, or a specialized organization, connecting with like-minded individuals can be immensely beneficial.

4. Utilize professional resources: Don't hesitate to seek professional help when needed. Therapists, counselors, or coaches can offer specialized guidance and support in navigating challenges. They can provide a safe and confidential space for exploring your thoughts and emotions and offer effective strategies for coping with difficulties.

5. Regularly connect and check-in: Maintain regular communication with your support network. Schedule time for social interactions, whether it's meeting up in person, video calls, or regular check-ins through phone or messaging apps. Cultivate a sense of connection and ongoing support by staying engaged with the individuals in your network.

Remember, everyone's journey is unique, and setbacks are a natural part of life. By implementing these coping strategies and leaning on your support network, you can navigate challenges with greater resilience and emerge stronger on the other side.

Cultivating Confidence Through Self-Love

Are you ready to unleash your confidence? It's time to break free from self-doubt and embrace your worth! Building confidence in women is an empowering journey that starts with self-love. When women cultivate self-love, they develop a deep appreciation for their unique qualities, strengths, and beauty. It's about accepting yourself as you are, celebrating your imperfections, and treating yourself with kindness and respect.

Self-doubt and potential both play significant roles in the development of self-confidence. Here's how they relate. Self-doubt refers to the lack of belief in your abilities, worth, or potential, and by now, you should know all about your amazing-ness! Self-doubt often manifests as negative self-talk, questioning one's capabilities, or fearing failure. Self-doubt can be a significant obstacle to building self-confidence because it undermines belief in yourself.

Overcoming self-doubt is essential for building self-confidence. It involves challenging negative self-perceptions, reframing limiting beliefs, and developing a more positive and realistic self-image. Recognizing that self-doubt is a normal part of the human experience and not an accurate reflection of one's abilities is crucial. By practicing self-compassion, cultivating a growth mindset, and focusing on personal growth and progress, individuals can gradually overcome self-doubt and nurture self-confidence. You got the tools girl, and it's time to use them!

The other way you're gonna build that shining confidence is by embracing your potential. It's about recognizing and acknowledging the inherent abilities, talents, and strengths that reside within you. Embracing potential means shifting from a mindset of limitations to a mindset of possibilities, otherwise known as….take a guess….growth mindset!

Self-confidence grows when you recognize and tap into your potential. By setting achievable goals, taking small steps towards personal growth, and celebrating successes along the way, you can build confidence in your abilities. Embracing potential allows you to stretch beyond your comfort zones, take risks, and believe in your capacity to handle challenges and setbacks.

Self-doubt and potential often operate in a feedback loop. When self-doubt dominates, it can hinder you from fully embracing your potential. Conversely, when you recognize and embrace your potential, it can help alleviate self-doubt and boost self-confidence. As you develop confidence in your abilities, you'll become more resilient in the face of challenges and setbacks, which further reinforces their belief in their potential. Double knockout!

Ultimately, overcoming self-doubt and embracing your potential are integral to developing self-confidence. By challenging negative self-perceptions, nurturing self-compassion, and actively pursuing personal growth, you can cultivate a stronger sense of confidence and belief in yourself. Hoorah!

Building Resilience

We've touched on this lightly, but it's time to get into all the juicy details. So let's talk about it. Well, I'll write, you read about it. Learning from failures and adapting to change are crucial components in building resilience. Resilience is the ability to bounce back from setbacks, adapt to challenges, and continue moving forward.

When we approach failures as opportunities for growth rather than as personal shortcomings, we cultivate a growth mindset; bingo, there it is again! By viewing failures as stepping stones to success, we develop the resilience to persevere and try again.

Okay so you already know about the growth mindset; fine. But another key component is adaptability. Change is inevitable in life, and developing the ability to adapt is key to building resilience. Adapting to change requires flexibility, open-mindedness, and a willingness to step out of our comfort zones. It involves embracing new perspectives, adjusting our plans, and seeking alternative solutions. By embracing change and being adaptable, we become better equipped to navigate unexpected challenges and bounce back stronger.

Resilience also involves developing effective problem-solving skills. When faced with obstacles, resilient individuals approach them with a proactive mindset. They analyze the situation, identify potential solutions, and take action. By actively engaging in problem-solving, we build confidence in our ability to overcome challenges, which further strengthens our resilience.

Remember, building resilience is a journey that requires practice and patience. By learning from failures, adapting to change, and cultivating a growth mindset, you can develop the resilience needed to navigate life's ups and downs with greater strength and confidence.

Leaving a Legacy of Self-Love

Alright, folks, we've reached the grand finale of our self-love journey: leaving a legacy of self-love! It's time to unleash our inner superheroes and empower future generations of women with all the wisdom and self-love we've gathered throughout this book. So grab your capes and let's dive in!

By applying everything we've learned about self-love, we have the power to create a ripple effect that will touch the lives of those around us, including our daughters, nieces, sisters, and friends. Imagine a world where self-love is not just a buzzword, but a way of life for women everywhere. Now that's a legacy worth leaving!

So, how can we empower future generations through our self-love journey? Let's break it down:

1. Lead by example: The most powerful way to inspire others is by living our own lives authentically and unapologetically. Show the world what it means to embrace your flaws, celebrate your achievements, and prioritize self-care. Be a shining example of self-love, and others will be drawn to your radiance.

2. Teach the next generation: Share your self-love journey with the young women in your life. Talk openly about the importance of self-worth, setting boundaries, embracing imperfections, and practicing self-care. Educate them about the power of self-love and equip them with the tools they need to navigate life with confidence and compassion.

3. Challenge stereotypes and break barriers: Empower future generations by challenging societal norms and stereotypes that limit women's potential. Encourage young girls to pursue their passions, dream big, and break free from the shackles of gender expectations. Let's create a world where every girl believes she can be anything she wants to be.

4. Celebrate diversity and inclusion: Embrace the beauty of diversity and teach future generations to do the same. Promote inclusivity, respect different perspectives, and stand up against discrimination. Let's create a world where all women feel seen, heard, and valued for who they are.

5. Spread kindness and lift others up: Support and uplift other women on their own self-love journeys. Share your experiences, offer a listening ear, and celebrate their achievements. Together, we can create a sisterhood of empowered women who lift each other up rather than tear each other down.

Remember, leaving a legacy of self-love is not about being perfect or having it all figured out. It's about embracing our own growth, learning from our mistakes, and inspiring others to do the same. So, let's go out there and make a lasting impact by spreading the message of self-love far and wide.

Conclusion

And with that, my friends, we conclude our incredible journey through the world of self-love. It has been an honor and a privilege to guide you on this adventure. Remember, you are worthy, you are deserving, and you are enough. Embrace your uniqueness, celebrate your journey, and continue to nourish your self-love flame.

Now go forth, my self-love warriors, and let's change the world one loving act at a time.

Takeaways

- Embrace vulnerability as a courageous act of authenticity and imperfection.
- Overcome setbacks and challenges by utilizing coping strategies and building a strong support network.
- Develop self-confidence by conquering self-doubt and embracing your potential.
- Cultivate resilience through learning from failures and adapting to change.
- Empower future generations of women by applying the principles of self-love and becoming a role model.
- Leave a legacy of self-love that inspires and uplifts others, creating a world where every woman embraces her worth and shines brightly.

EPILOGUE

"Self-love is the key to unlocking your true potential and embracing the extraordinary woman you are meant to be." - Unknown

In this epilogue, we take a moment to reflect on our self-love journey, to bask in the warmth of our growth, and to celebrate the incredible power of self-love for women. It has been a remarkable expedition, filled with laughter, tears, and countless aha moments. So let's take a deep breath, gather our thoughts, and indulge in a final chapter of this beautiful tale.

Throughout this book, we have explored the depths of self-love, unraveling its layers and discovering its transformative magic. We have learned that self-love is not a destination but a lifelong dance—a dance of embracing our imperfections, celebrating our victories, and nourishing our souls.

We have laughed together at our sarcastic remarks, held hands through the challenging moments, and shared the joy of self-discovery. We have dug deep into our hearts, facing fears, breaking free from societal expectations, and reclaiming our authentic selves.

In each chapter, we have woven a tapestry of self-love, intertwining the threads of compassion, acceptance, resilience, and empowerment. We have unearthed the power of setting boundaries, embracing vulnerability, and nurturing relationships. We have stood tall in the face of self-doubt, celebrated our unique strengths, and forged a path of self-confidence.

But our journey doesn't end here. No, dear reader, it's only the beginning. Armed with the tools, insights, and unwavering belief in ourselves, we step into the world with newfound clarity and purpose. We carry the torch of self-love, ready to inspire and ignite the flames of self-worth in others.

As we bid farewell to this book, let us remember that self-love is not a solitary endeavor. It's a collective movement, a ripple that spreads far and wide, transforming lives and shaping a future where every woman stands tall in her worth and radiates her unique brilliance.

So, my dear friend, take a moment to honor yourself. Celebrate the incredible journey you've embarked upon. And know that as you continue to nourish your self-love, you are not only changing your own life but also impacting the lives of those around you.

May self-love be your guiding light, your steadfast companion, and your unwavering source of strength. Embrace the beauty of your journey, for you are an embodiment of love, resilience, and endless possibilities.

FURTHER READING

1. *The Gifts of Imperfection* by Brené Brown: In this book, Brené Brown explores the power of embracing imperfections, cultivating self-compassion, and living wholeheartedly.

2. *Radical Acceptance: Embracing Your Life With the Heart of a Buddha* by Tara Brach: Tara Brach offers guidance on accepting ourselves and our life circumstances with compassion, mindfulness, and emotional healing.

3. *The Confidence Code: The Science and Art of Self-Assurance—What Women Should Know* by Katty Kay and Claire Shipman: This book explores the science behind confidence and offers practical strategies for women to develop and enhance their self-confidence.

4. *Daring Greatly: How the Courage to Be Vulnerable Transforms the Way We Live, Love, Parent, and Lead* by Brené Brown: Brené Brown delves into the power of vulnerability, challenging shame and fear, and embracing courageous living.

5. *Big Magic: Creative Living Beyond Fear* by Elizabeth Gilbert: This book encourages women to embrace their creativity, pursue their passions, and overcome self-doubt and fear in the creative process.

6. *The Four Agreements: A Practical Guide to Personal Freedom* by Don Miguel Ruiz: Don Miguel Ruiz presents four guiding principles for personal growth and transformation, promoting self-love, authenticity, and freedom.

7. *The Power of Now: A Guide to Spiritual Enlightenment* by Eckhart Tolle: This book explores the importance of living in the present moment, releasing past conditioning, and finding inner peace and fulfillment.

8. *Love Warrior: A Memoir* by Glennon Doyle: Glennon Doyle shares her personal journey of self-discovery, self-acceptance, and embracing vulnerability in relationships and personal growth.

9. *Untamed* by Glennon Doyle: In this book, Glennon Doyle challenges societal expectations, explores the power of intuition, and encourages women to reclaim their true selves.

10. *You Are a Badass: How to Stop Doubting Your Greatness and Start Living an Awesome Life* by Jen Sincero: This book provides motivational insights and practical strategies to overcome self-doubt, cultivate self-love, and create a life of fulfillment.

These books delve into various aspects of self-love, personal growth, vulnerability, confidence, and resilience, offering further exploration and inspiration for readers on their journey of self-discovery and empowerment.

REFERENCES

Baumeister, R. F., Campbell, J. D., Krueger, J. I., & Vohs, K. D. (2003). "Does high self-esteem cause better performance, interpersonal success, happiness, or healthier lifestyles?" *Psychological Science in the Public Interest, 4*(1), 1-44.

Blatt, S.J., Zuroff, D.C., Hawley, L.L., & Auerbach, J.S. (2010). "Predictors of sustained therapeutic change." *Psychother Res., 20*(1), 37-54.

Buchanan, K. E., & Bardi, A. (2010). "Acts of kindness and acts of novelty affect life satisfaction." *The Journal of Social Psychology, 150*(3), 235-237.

Clark, D. A., & Beck, A. T. (2011). "Cognitive theory and therapy of anxiety and depression: Convergence with neurobiological findings." *Trends in Cognitive Sciences, 16*(9), 533-540.

Dweck, C. S. (2006). *Mindset: The New Psychology of Success.* Random House.

Grabe, S., Ward, L. M., & Hyde, J. S. (2008). "The role of the media in body image concerns among women: A meta-analysis of experimental and correlational studies." *Sex Roles, 59*(1-2), 1-15.

Harvey, A. G., & Watkins, E. (2018). "Cognitive behavioral processes across psychological disorders: A review of the utility and specificity of the transdiagnostic approach." *International Journal of Cognitive Therapy, 11*(3), 216-234.

Huang, X., Dong, Y., Lu, Y., & Ai, Z. (2019). "Self-love, self-esteem, and life satisfaction: The mediating role of psychological resilience." *Journal of Health Psychology, 24*(3), 290-299.

Konrath, S. H., Meier, B. P., & Bushman, B. J. (2014). "Development and validation of the Narcissistic Personality Inventory–16 (NPI-16)." *Journal of Personality Assessment, 96*(3), 253-260.

Kruger, J., & Dunning, D. (1999). "Unskilled and unaware of it: How difficulties in recognizing one's own incompetence lead to inflated self-assessments." *Journal of Personality and Social Psychology, 77*(6), 1121–1134.

Neff, K. D., & McGehee, P. (2010). "Self-compassion and psychological resilience among adolescents and young adults." *Self and Identity, 9*(3), 225-240.

Sharma, N. (2013). "The work-family interface and well-being: A study of Indian working women." *Journal of Family Issues, 34*(1), 75-96.

Simpson, J. A., Collins, W. A., Tran, S., & Haydon, K. C. (2007). "Attachment and the experience and expression of emotions in romantic relationships: A developmental perspective." *Journal of Personality and Social Psychology, 92*(2), 355-367.

Smith, S. L., Choueiti, M., & Pieper, K. (2013). *Gender bias without borders: An investigation of female characters in popular films across 11 countries.* Los Angeles, CA: Geena Davis Institute on Gender in Media.

Smith, J., & Hughes, J. (2019). "The impact of work-life balance on wellbeing: Evidence from the UK." *Social Indicators Research, 141*(2), 661–688.

Tangney, J.P., Stuewig, J., & Mashek, D.J. (2007). "Moral emotions and moral behavior." *Annual Review of Psychology, 58*(1), 345-372.

Vogel, E. A., Rose, J. P., Roberts, L. R., & Eckles, K. (2014). "Social comparison, social media, and self-esteem." *Psychology of Popular Media Culture, 3*(4), 206-222.

World Health Organization. (2013). *Global and regional estimates of violence against women: Prevalence and health effects of intimate partner violence and non-partner sexual violence.*

Made in the USA
Las Vegas, NV
24 April 2024

89079326R00094